BEST MOVIES OF ALL TIME IN A SENTENCE

THE 1000 FILMS THAT YOU SHOULD WATCH IMMEDIATELY, SIMPLY EXPLAINED

NO-BRAINER BOOKS

CONTENTS

1) The Shawshank Redemption

The Shawshank Redemption is a classic prison drama about the power of hope, friendship, and resilience in the face of overwhelming odds.

2) The Godfather

The Godfather is a classic crime drama about a mafia family's struggle for power and respect in 1950s America.

3) The Dark Knight

The Dark Knight is a thrilling action-packed superhero movie about the battle between Batman and The Joker for control of Gotham City.

4) Schindler's List

Schindler's List is a powerful and emotionally moving film about the Holocaust, depicting Oskar Schindler's heroic efforts to save the lives of his Jewish workers.

5) The Godfather: Part II

The Godfather: Part II follows the story of Michael Corleone, the new Don of the Corleone family, as he attempts to expand the family's criminal empire while dealing with the consequences of his actions.

6) 12 Angry Men

Twelve jurors must decide the fate of a young man accused of murder, and through a series of heated debates, come to understand the power of justice and the importance of reasonable doubt.

7) The Lord of the Rings: The Return of the King

The Lord of the Rings: The Return of the King follows the heroic quest of Frodo and his companions as they battle to save Middle-earth from the forces of the Dark Lord Sauron.

8) Pulp Fiction

Pulp Fiction is a darkly comic crime film that follows the intersecting lives of two mob hitmen, a boxer, a gangster's wife, and a pair of diner bandits.

9) 777 Charlie

777 Charlie is a heartwarming adventure about a boy and his loyal dog's journey to reunite with their family.

10) Inception

Inception is a thrilling science fiction film about a team of criminals who use dream-sharing technology to pull off a heist of corporate secrets from the subconscious mind of a target.

11) Fight Club

Fight Club is a darkly comedic, psychological drama about a man's transformation from a bored, white-collar worker to an anarchic, nihilistic cult leader.

12) The Lord of the Rings: The Fellowship of the Ring

The Lord of the Rings: The Fellowship of the Ring follows the quest of a fellowship of hobbits, elves, dwarves, and humans to destroy the One Ring and save Middle-earth from the evil forces of Sauron.

13) Forrest Gump

Forrest Gump is a heartwarming story of an innocent man's journey through life, showing that love and determination can conquer all.

14) The Good, the Bad and the Ugly

The Good, the Bad and the Ugly is a classic spaghetti western that follows three gunslingers as they search for a hidden fortune during the American Civil War.

15) The Lord of the Rings: The Two Towers

The Lord of the Rings: The Two Towers is an epic fantasy adventure film that follows the continuing quest of Frodo and Sam to destroy the One Ring and stand against the evil forces of Sauron.

16) Jai Bhim

Jai Bhim is a documentary about the struggles and triumphs of Dalit communities in India, highlighting the story of Dr. Bhimrao Ambedkar, the leader of the Dalit movement.

17) Rocketry: The Nambi Effect

Rocketry: The Nambi Effect is a biographical drama about the life of Indian aerospace engineer Nambi Narayanan, who was falsely accused of espionage and fought for justice.

18) Goodfellas

Goodfellas is a classic crime drama about a group of gangsters in New York City and their rise and fall in the mob world.

19) The Matrix

The Matrix is a sci-fi action movie about a computer hacker who discovers the world he lives in is a simulated reality created by machines.

20) One Flew Over the Cuckoo's Nest

One Flew Over the Cuckoo's Nest is a 1975 American drama film about a criminal who is sent to a mental institution and attempts to lead its inmates in a revolt against the oppressive and abusive staff.

21) Star Wars: Episode V - The Empire Strikes Back

The Empire Strikes Back is an epic space opera that follows the heroes of the Rebel Alliance as they battle the Galactic Empire, led by Darth Vader, in a struggle for freedom.

22) Soorarai Pottru

Soorarai Pottru is a heartwarming story of an underdog's struggle to fulfill his dream of starting an airline in India.

23) Interstellar

Interstellar is a science fiction epic that follows a team of astronauts as they travel through a wormhole in search of a new home for humanity.

24) Se7en

Se7en is a crime thriller about two detectives trying to catch a serial killer who uses the seven deadly sins as his modus operandi.

25) Life Is Beautiful

Life Is Beautiful is a heartwarming and humorous story of a father's love and courage in the face of tragedy during World War II.

26) The Green Mile

The Green Mile is a drama about a prison guard who develops a strong bond with an inmate on death row who possesses a magical gift.

27) The Silence of the Lambs

The Silence of the Lambs is a psychological thriller about a young FBI cadet's attempt to catch a serial killer with the help of an imprisoned cannibalistic psychiatrist.

28) Star Wars: Episode IV - A New Hope

Star Wars: Episode IV - A New Hope is an epic space opera that follows a young farm boy, Luke Skywalker, as he joins forces with a Jedi Knight and two droids to save the galaxy from the evil Galactic Empire.

29) Saving Private Ryan

Saving Private Ryan follows a group of World War II soldiers on a mission to find and save the last surviving brother of a family of soldiers.

30) Terminator 2: Judgment Day

Terminator 2: Judgment Day is a sci-fi action movie in which a cyborg is sent back in time to protect John Connor from a more advanced Terminator sent to kill him.

31) Spirited Away

Spirited Away is an animated fantasy adventure film about a young girl who must find a way to free herself and her parents from a spirit world.

32) City of God

City of God is a gripping Brazilian crime drama that follows two boys growing up in a violent Rio de Janeiro favela.

33) It's a Wonderful Life

It's a Wonderful Life is a classic Christmas movie about a man who learns the value of his life and the impact he has had on others after being shown what the world would be like if he had never been born.

34) Seven Samurai

Seven Samurai is a classic Japanese epic about a group of masterless samurai who are hired to defend a small village from a band of marauding bandits.

35) Sita Ramam

Sita Ramam is a classic Indian drama that follows the story of a young woman's journey of self-discovery as she struggles to balance her traditional roots with modern society.

36) Harakiri

Harakiri is a Japanese samurai drama about a ronin who seeks to commit ritual suicide in order to restore his honor.

37) Whiplash

Whiplash is a drama about a young jazz drummer's passionate pursuit of greatness that leads to an intense mentor-mentee relationship with a demanding music teacher.

38) Parasite

Parasite is a darkly comedic and socially relevant story of two families from different classes whose lives become intertwined with unexpected consequences.

39) The Prestige

The Prestige is a thrilling drama about two rival magicians who will go to extreme lengths to outdo each other in a deadly battle of deception and trickery.

40) The Departed

The Departed is a crime drama about an undercover cop and a criminal infiltrating the Massachusetts State Police and the Irish Mob, respectively, in a deadly game of cat and mouse.

41) Léon: The Professional

Léon: The Professional is an action-packed crime drama about a professional hitman who takes a young girl under his wing and helps her avenge her family's death.

42) Gladiator

Gladiator is a 2000 historical epic drama film about a Roman general who is betrayed and forced into slavery, who then rises through the ranks of the gladiatorial arena to avenge the murder of his family.

43) Apocalypse Now

Apocalypse Now is a psychological war drama that follows an Army Captain's journey into the depths of the Vietnam War to find and kill a renegade American colonel.

44) Alien

Alien is a classic sci-fi horror movie about a group of space travelers who must fight for their lives against a terrifying extraterrestrial creature.

45) Back to the Future

Back to the Future is a classic time-traveling adventure comedy about a teenager and a mad scientist who travel back in time to 1955 in a DeLorean.

46) The Usual Suspects

The Usual Suspects is a neo-noir mystery film about a group of criminals who are drawn into a complex web of deception and intrigue.

47) American History X

American History X is a powerful drama about a reformed neo-Nazi's attempt to prevent his younger brother from going down the same hate-filled path.

48) The Lion King

The Lion King is an animated classic about a young lion cub's journey to adulthood as he struggles to accept the responsibilities of being the future king.

49) The Pianist

The Pianist is a powerful and emotional story about a Jewish pianist's struggle to survive the Holocaust in Nazi-occupied Poland.

50) The Intouchables

The Intouchables is a heartwarming story of friendship between a wealthy, paralyzed aristocrat and his ex-convict caretaker.

51) Once Upon a Time in the West

Once Upon a Time in the West is a classic western set in the American Old West, following a mysterious gunslinger as he attempts to protect a woman from a ruthless robber baron.

52) Casablanca

Set in World War II-era Morocco, Casablanca is a romantic drama about a man torn between love and virtue in a world of political turmoil.

53) Psycho

Psycho is a classic Hitchcock thriller about a motel owner with a dark past who goes to extreme lengths to protect his secrets.

54) Grave of the Fireflies

Grave of the Fireflies is an emotionally powerful and heartbreaking story of two siblings struggling to survive during the final months of World War II in Japan.

55) Cinema Paradiso

Cinema Paradiso is a heartwarming story of a young boy's love of film and his lifelong friendship with the projectionist at his small-town cinema.

56) Rear Window

Rear Window follows a wheelchair-bound photographer who spies on his neighbors and becomes convinced one of them has committed murder.

57) Modern Times

Modern Times is a classic silent comedy about a factory worker's struggle to stay sane in a modern, industrialized world.

58) Kaithi

Kaithi is an action-packed thriller that follows a former convict on a mission to save his daughter from a dangerous drug lord.

59) City Lights

City Lights is a romantic comedy-drama about a tramp who falls in love with a blind flower girl and struggles to raise money for her eye operation.

60) 96

96 is a romantic drama about two former high school sweethearts who reunite after a long separation and must reconcile the past with their present lives.

61) Avengers: Endgame

The Avengers must use their newfound powers and resources to reverse Thanos' destruction and restore balance to the universe.

62) Joker

Joker is a dark psychological drama about a failed comedian's descent into madness as he transforms into the infamous villain.

63) Indiana Jones and the Raiders of the Lost Ark

Indiana Jones embarks on an adventurous quest to find the ancient and powerful artifact, the Ark of the Covenant, before it falls into the hands of the Nazis.

64) Django Unchained

Django Unchained is a Western revenge film that follows a freed slave's quest to rescue his wife from a cruel plantation owner.

65) American Beauty

American Beauty is a darkly comedic drama about a middle-aged man's mid-life crisis and his dysfunctional family's attempts to cope with it.

66) The Dark Knight Rises

The Dark Knight Rises is a thrilling conclusion to Christopher Nolan's Batman trilogy, in which Bruce Wayne must face his greatest challenge yet.

67) Memento

Memento is a psychological thriller about a man trying to find the person responsible for the death of his wife while suffering from anterograde amnesia.

68) Aliens

Aliens follows Ellen Ripley as she returns to the alien planet with a team of marines to confront the hostile extraterrestrials and their queen.

69) Avengers: Infinity War

The Avengers must unite to stop Thanos from collecting the Infinity Stones and wiping out half of the universe.

70) Oldboy

Oldboy is a dark and violent revenge thriller about a man who is mysteriously imprisoned for 15 years and must uncover the reason for his captivity in order to gain his freedom.

71) The Shining

The Shining is a psychological horror film about a family who is terrorized by supernatural forces while staying in a secluded hotel.

72) Spider-Man: Into the Spider-Verse

Spider-Man: Into the Spider-Verse follows the story of Miles Morales as he teams up with other versions of Spider-Man from alternate dimensions to save New York City.

73) Kantara

Kantara is a drama about a young woman's journey of self-discovery and reconciliation with her past, as she comes to terms with the consequences of her actions and learns to forgive herself.

74) Amadeus

Amadeus is a biographical drama about the life and career of legendary composer Wolfgang

Amadeus Mozart, as told from the perspective of his jealous rival Antonio Salieri.

75) Braveheart

Braveheart is a 1995 epic historical drama film about the 13th-century Scottish warrior William Wallace and his fight for independence from England.

76) Come and See

Come and See is a powerful and haunting war drama about a young Belarusian boy's journey through the horrors of World War II.

77) Hamilton

Hamilton is a musical biopic about the life of American Founding Father Alexander Hamilton, which tells the story of his rise from poverty to power through a blend of traditional musical theater and hip-hop.

78) Coco

Coco is a heartwarming story of a young boy's journey through the Land of the Dead to discover his family's musical legacy.

79) Your Name.

Your Name is a Japanese animated film about two high schoolers who mysteriously switch bodies and embark on a journey to find each other.

80) 3 Idiots

3 Idiots is a heartwarming comedy-drama about three friends who embark on a journey of self-discovery and challenge the status quo of their traditional Indian society.

81) WALL·E

WALL·E is a heartwarming animated film about a lonely robot who embarks on an adventure to save humanity and the planet.

82) The Lives of Others

The Lives of Others is a powerful drama about a Stasi agent who is assigned to spy on a talented East German playwright and his lover, and is ultimately changed by the experience.

83) Capernaum

Capernaum is a heartbreaking story of a young boy's struggle against the injustice of poverty and neglect in modern-day Lebanon.

84) Princess Mononoke

Princess Mononoke is an epic fantasy adventure film about a young warrior's fight to protect a sacred forest from the destruction of humans.

85) Dr. Strangelove or: How I Learned to Stop Worrying and Love the Bomb

Dr. Strangelove is a satirical dark comedy about a group of military leaders who attempt to prevent a nuclear apocalypse, but ultimately fail.

86) The Boat

The Boat is a drama about a German family struggling to survive during World War II, and the sacrifices they must make for freedom.

87) Witness for the Prosecution

Witness for the Prosecution is a courtroom drama about a man on trial for murder who is defended by a brilliant lawyer who is determined to prove his innocence.

88) Sunset Blvd.

Sunset Blvd. is a 1950's film noir about a faded silent-screen star who takes a screenwriter under her wing as her life spirals out of control.

89) Paths of Glory

Paths of Glory is a powerful anti-war film about a French colonel who defends three innocent soldiers accused of cowardice during World War I.

90) Drishyam 2

Drishyam 2 follows the story of Georgekutty and his family as they attempt to outsmart the law and prove their innocence in the face of a murder investigation.

91) The Great Dictator

The Great Dictator is a 1940 satirical comedy-drama film about a Jewish barber who is mistaken for a tyrannical dictator and must take a stand against the oppressive regime.

92) High and Low

High and Low is a crime drama about a wealthy businessman who is forced to make a difficult decision when a criminal kidnaps his son for ransom.

93) Shershaah

Shershaah is a biographical war drama based on the life of Indian Army officer and war hero Vikram Batra, who sacrificed his life in the Kargil War of 1999.

94) Sardar Udham

Sardar Udham is a 2020 Indian action-drama film about a man who seeks revenge against the people responsible for the death of his father and the destruction of his village.

95) Asuran

Asuran is a Tamil-language action drama film about a young man who seeks revenge against a powerful landlord after his father is wrongfully killed.

96) Top Gun: Maverick

Top Gun: Maverick is a sequel to the 1986 classic, following the story of an elite fighter pilot who is pushed to his limits as he confronts the ghosts of his past.

97) Good Will Hunting

Good Will Hunting is a drama about a troubled young man from a working-class background who is discovered to have a genius-level intellect and is mentored by a therapist to help him reach his full potential.

98) Heat

Heat is a crime drama that follows a group of professional criminals and the determined detective who is determined to bring them to justice.

99) Inglourious Basterds

Inglourious Basterds is a World War II-era action-adventure film about a group of Jewish-American soldiers on a mission to kill Nazis in France.

100) Requiem for a Dream

Requiem for a Dream is a tragic story of four characters whose lives spiral out of control due to their addiction to drugs.

101) Reservoir Dogs

Reservoir Dogs is a crime thriller about a group of criminals who attempt to pull off a diamond heist, but are ultimately betrayed by one of their own.

102) Eternal Sunshine of the Spotless Mind

Eternal Sunshine of the Spotless Mind is a romantic drama about a couple who erase each other from their memories after a painful breakup, only to realize they still have feelings for each other.

103) The Sting

The Sting is a 1973 crime caper film about two con men who attempt to pull off the ultimate con on a mob boss.

104) Scarface

Scarface is a crime drama about a Cuban immigrant's rise to power in the Miami drug scene.

105) A Clockwork Orange

A Clockwork Orange is a dystopian crime film that follows the violent exploits of a young delinquent and his eventual redemption.

106) The Hunt

The Hunt follows a group of strangers who are mysteriously chosen to participate in a twisted game of survival.

107) 2001: A Space Odyssey

2001: A Space Odyssey is a sci-fi classic that follows a voyage to Jupiter as a mysterious monolith transforms the lives of a crew of astronauts and a sentient computer.

108) Full Metal Jacket

Full Metal Jacket is a darkly humorous war film that follows a group of Marines through their rigorous training and subsequent deployment to Vietnam.

109) Once Upon a Time in America

Once Upon a Time in America is an epic crime drama that follows the lives of Jewish gangsters in New York City from their youth in the 1920s to their eventual downfall in the 1960s.

110) Toy Story

Toy Story is an animated adventure about the friendship between a group of toys that come to life when humans are not around.

111) Star Wars: Episode VI - Return of the Jedi

In the epic conclusion of the original Star Wars trilogy, Luke Skywalker and his allies face off against the Galactic Empire in a climactic battle to restore peace and freedom to the galaxy.

112) Amélie

Amélie is a whimsical romantic comedy about a shy waitress in Paris who discovers her purpose in life by helping others find happiness.

113) Incendies

Incendies is a powerful and emotionally charged drama about a brother and sister's journey to uncover their mother's mysterious past in the Middle East.

114) Up

A grumpy old man and a young boy embark on an adventure of a lifetime when they tie thousands of balloons to the old man's house and fly to South America.

115) Lawrence of Arabia

Lawrence of Arabia is an epic historical drama that follows the story of T.E. Lawrence, a British Army officer who unites the diverse, warring Arab tribes during World War I to fight the Ottoman Empire.

116) Citizen Kane

Citizen Kane is a classic film about a powerful newspaper tycoon whose life and legacy are explored through a series of flashbacks.

117) Toy Story 3

Toy Story 3 follows the beloved characters of the Toy Story franchise as they go on an emotional journey of self-discovery and acceptance.

118) Vertigo

Vertigo follows the story of a man struggling with his fear of heights and obsession with a woman who appears to have a mysterious past.

119) North by Northwest

North by Northwest is a classic Hitchcock thriller about a man who is mistaken for a spy and must evade the police and a mysterious group of criminals.

120) Metropolis

Metropolis is a science fiction film set in a futuristic city, depicting a struggle between the city's working class and its ruling class.

121) Singin' in the Rain

Singin' in the Rain is a classic musical comedy about two actors navigating the transition from silent film to talking pictures in 1920s Hollywood.

122) To Kill a Mockingbird

To Kill a Mockingbird is a classic story of injustice and courage set in the Deep South during the Great Depression.

123) Judgment at Nuremberg

Judgment at Nuremberg is a thought-provoking courtroom drama that examines the morality of the post-WWII trials of Nazi war criminals.

124) The Apartment

The Apartment is a romantic comedy-drama about a man who lends out his apartment to his superiors for their extramarital affairs, only to find himself falling for one of the women involved.

125) Dangal

Dangal is a heartwarming Indian sports drama about a father who trains his daughters to become world-class wrestlers.

126) A Separation

A Separation is a powerful drama that follows a married couple in Iran as they face a difficult decision that leads to a tumultuous journey of self-discovery and moral conflict.

127) M

M is a 1931 German drama film directed by Fritz Lang that follows the investigations of a police inspector into a child murderer in Berlin.

128) Ikiru

Ikiru is a Japanese drama film about a middle-aged bureaucrat who embarks on a journey of self-discovery and redemption after being diagnosed with terminal cancer.

129) Vikram

Vikram is a thrilling action-packed drama that follows a police officer as he attempts to bring justice to a corrupt society.

130) K.G.F: Chapter 2

K.G.F: Chapter 2 is a 2019 Indian period action film that follows the story of a young man's journey to fulfill his ambition of becoming the most powerful man in the world.

131) Double Indemnity

Double Indemnity is a 1944 film noir about an insurance salesman and a femme fatale who conspire to commit murder for the sake of a hefty insurance payout.

132) Like Stars on Earth

Like Stars on Earth is a heartwarming story about a struggling student who discovers his true potential with the help of an understanding teacher.

133) Bicycle Thieves

Bicycle Thieves is a neorealist drama about a man and his son searching for a stolen bicycle in post-WWII Rome which serves as a metaphor for the desperate struggle of the working class.

134) The Kid

The Kid is a comedy-drama about a young boy's journey to find his place in the world.

135) Ayla: The Daughter of War

Ayla: The Daughter of War is a heart-wrenching story of a Turkish soldier who forms an unlikely bond with an orphaned Kurdish girl during the Korean War.

136) Drishyam

Drishyam is a gripping thriller about a family man who goes to great lengths to protect his family from the law.

137) Pather Panchali

Pather Panchali is a Bengali film that follows the life of a family living in a rural village in Bengal, India, and the struggles they face in their everyday lives.

138) Raatchasan

Raatchasan is a psychological thriller that follows a police officer as he attempts to track down a serial killer preying on young women.

139) Chhichhore

Chhichhore is a coming-of-age story about a group of friends who reunite after years apart to relive fond memories and ultimately find closure.

140) Spider-Man: No Way Home

Spider-Man: No Way Home follows Peter Parker and his friends as they face new challenges and unexpected villains while navigating their complicated lives in a multiverse of alternate realities.

141) The Wolf of Wall Street

The Wolf of Wall Street is a black comedy-drama film about the rise and fall of stockbroker

Jordan Belfort, whose career is fueled by greed and excess.

142) Jurassic Park

Jurassic Park is a thrilling adventure film about a group of people who must survive on an island populated with dinosaurs created by a billionaire's dangerous experiment.

143) Green Book

Green Book is a heartwarming story of an unlikely friendship between a working-class Italian-American bouncer and an African-American classical pianist on a tour of the segregated Deep South in the early 1960s.

144) Shutter Island

Shutter Island is a psychological thriller about an U.S. Marshal investigating the disappearance of a patient from a hospital for the criminally insane on an island off the coast of Massachusetts.

145) No Country for Old Men

No Country for Old Men is a dark, suspenseful crime drama that follows a hunter who stumbles upon a drug deal gone wrong and the ensuing chaos that ensues.

146) Taxi Driver

Taxi Driver is a psychological drama about a disturbed Vietnam veteran who descends into a violent obsession with saving a young prostitute.

147) 1917

1917 is a thrilling and heart-wrenching war drama that follows two British soldiers on a seemingly impossible mission to save 1,600 of their fellow troops.

148) The Father

The Father is a heart-wrenching drama about a man struggling with the challenges of dementia, and the impact it has on his relationships with his daughter and the people around him.

149) Indiana Jones and the Last Crusade

Indiana Jones embarks on a dangerous quest to find the elusive Holy Grail and save his father from the Nazis.

150) Snatch

Snatch is a crime comedy about a diamond heist gone wrong, set in the London underworld.

151) Batman Begins

Batman Begins is a superhero film that follows Bruce Wayne as he embarks on a journey of self-discovery, as he learns to become the Dark Knight of Gotham City.

152) The Truman Show

The Truman Show is a 1998 film about a man who is unknowingly living in a constructed reality television show, unaware that his entire life is being broadcast to the world.

153) The Sixth Sense

The Sixth Sense is a psychological thriller about a young boy who can see and talk to the dead.

154) Die Hard

Die Hard is an action-packed classic about an off-duty cop who must save his wife and other hostages from a group of terrorists in a high-rise office building.

155) Kill Bill: Vol. 1

Kill Bill: Vol. 1 is a revenge-filled action movie about a bride seeking to exact revenge on her former associates for attempting to murder her on her wedding day.

156) There Will Be Blood

There Will Be Blood is a drama about a ruthless oil tycoon's rise to power and the consequences of his ambition.

157) The Thing

The Thing follows a group of researchers in Antarctica as they are terrorized by a shape-shifting alien that has infiltrated their camp.

158) Finding Nemo

Finding Nemo is an animated adventure comedy about a clownfish father's journey to reunite with his son, who has been taken far from home.

159) Casino

Casino is a movie about the rise and fall of a Las Vegas mobster, and his struggle to maintain control of his casino empire amidst violence and betrayal.

160) Inside Out

Inside Out is an animated comedy-drama film that follows 11-year-old Riley as she navigates a difficult transition in her life, all while her emotions struggle to make sense of it all.

161) Chinatown

Chinatown is a neo-noir mystery film about a private investigator who uncovers a dark conspiracy involving the corruption of the city's water supply.

162) Howl's Moving Castle

Howl's Moving Castle is a fantasy adventure film about a young girl who is transformed into an old woman and must seek the help of a wizard to break the curse.

163) Pan's Labyrinth

Pan's Labyrinth is a dark fantasy film about a young girl who must confront both the real world and a mythical world in order to find her true destiny.

164) Lock, Stock and Two Smoking Barrels

Lock, Stock and Two Smoking Barrels is a British crime comedy about a group of friends who get caught up in a botched card game that results in a series of misadventures.

165) A Beautiful Mind

A Beautiful Mind is a biographical drama about a genius mathematician who battles schizophrenia and ultimately wins a Nobel Prize.

166) Warrior

Warrior is a powerful story of two estranged brothers who must overcome their differences to compete in an intense mixed martial arts tournament.

167) Gone with the Wind

Gone with the Wind is a classic epic romance set in the American Civil War, following the story of Scarlett O'Hara and her tumultuous journey of growth and love.

168) L.A. Confidential

L.A. Confidential is a neo-noir crime drama set in 1950s Los Angeles that follows three police officers as they investigate a series of murders while uncovering a web of corruption and deceit.

169) V for Vendetta

V for Vendetta is a dystopian political thriller about a mysterious freedom fighter who attempts to ignite a revolution against an oppressive government.

170) Unforgiven

Unforgiven is a Western drama about a retired gunslinger who is forced to take up arms one last time to seek revenge for a brutal act of injustice.

171) Downfall

Downfall is a German war drama about the last days of Adolf Hitler and the Nazi regime in 1945.

172) Some Like It Hot

Some Like It Hot is a classic romantic comedy about two male musicians who disguise themselves as women to escape from the mob and find themselves in a love triangle.

173) Drishyam

Drishyam is a gripping thriller about a man who goes to great lengths to protect his family from a ruthless police investigation.

174) Raging Bull

Raging Bull is a biographical drama about the life of boxer Jake LaMotta, whose self-destructive and obsessive rage ultimately leads to his downfall.

175) Monty Python and the Holy Grail

Monty Python and the Holy Grail is a comedic British film about King Arthur and his knights on a quest to find the Holy Grail.

176) The Secret in Their Eyes

The Secret in Their Eyes is a gripping crime drama that follows a retired criminal investigator's 25-year search for justice for a woman he loved.

177) The Elephant Man

The Elephant Man is a biographical drama about a severely deformed man who is mistreated and exploited until he is rescued by a doctor who strives to better his quality of life.

178) The Great Escape

The Great Escape is a classic World War II film about a group of Allied prisoners of war who plan an elaborate escape from a German POW camp.

179) Klaus

Klaus is an animated comedy-drama about a postman and a reclusive toymaker who form an unlikely friendship and bring joy and laughter to a small, Scandinavian town.

180) For a Few Dollars More

For a Few Dollars More is a classic western starring Clint Eastwood and Lee Van Cleef as two bounty hunters on a mission to take down a notorious criminal.

181) Ran

Ran is a Japanese period drama film that tells the story of a warlord's descent into madness after abdicating his throne to his three sons.

182) Tumbbad

Tumbbad is a dark fantasy horror film about a family cursed by an ancient entity and their desperate attempts to break free of its grasp.

183) Demon Slayer the Movie: Mugen Train

Demon Slayer the Movie: Mugen Train follows Tanjiro and his friends as they embark on a dangerous mission to investigate a mysterious series of disappearances occurring on a mysterious train.

184) The Bridge on the River Kwai

The Bridge on the River Kwai is a classic World War II drama about a group of British prisoners of war who are forced to build a bridge for their Japanese captors while also struggling to maintain their sense of honor and dignity.

185) Baahubali 2: The Conclusion

Baahubali 2: The Conclusion is an epic Indian fantasy action film that follows the story of the heroic prince, Shivudu, as he attempts to save his kingdom from the tyrannical rule of his uncle, Bhallaladeva.

186) Rashomon

Rashomon is a Japanese film that tells the story of a crime from four different perspectives, exploring the nature of truth and the human condition.

187) Dial M for Murder

Dial M for Murder is a classic Alfred Hitchcock thriller about a man who plots to have his wife murdered in order to gain her fortune.

188) All About Eve

All About Eve is a classic 1950s drama about an ambitious young actress who schemes her way into the life of a Broadway star.

189) The Treasure of the Sierra Madre

The Treasure of the Sierra Madre is a classic Western about two Americans and an old prospector who embark on a search for gold in the Mexican mountains, only to find themselves overcome by greed and distrust.

190) Gangs of Wasseypur

Gangs of Wasseypur is an Indian crime drama film that follows the generations of a family involved in a power struggle for control of the coal-mining town of Wasseypur.

191) Miracle in Cell No. 7

Miracle in Cell No. 7 is a heartwarming story about a father and daughter's bond, as he is wrongly convicted of a crime and sent to prison.

192) Andhadhun

Andhadhun is a dark comedy-thriller about a blind pianist who unknowingly becomes embroiled in a complex murder plot.

193) Yojimbo

Yojimbo is a 1961 Japanese samurai film about a ronin who arrives in a small town where two rival gangs are vying for control and must use his wits and skills to outwit them.

194) Tokyo Story

Tokyo Story is a heartbreaking yet beautiful story about an elderly couple visiting their grown children in Tokyo, only to find that their children have little time for them.

195) Children of Heaven

The Children of Heaven is a heartwarming story of two siblings who must share a single pair of shoes as they try to keep their family together in the face of poverty.

196) Z

Z is a political drama about a military commander who is determined to uncover the truth behind a mysterious assassination.

197) K.G.F: Chapter 1

K.G.F: Chapter 1 is a 2018 Indian action-drama film about a young man's journey to gain power and wealth in the ruthless world of Kolar Gold Fields.

198) Zindagi Na Milegi Dobara

Zindagi Na Milegi Dobara is a story about three friends who take a road trip to Spain and discover themselves along the way.

199) To Be or Not to Be

To Be or Not to Be is a black comedy about a troupe of actors in Nazi-occupied Poland who use their acting skills to fool the Nazis and save their lives.

200) The Passion of Joan of Arc

The Passion of Joan of Arc is a silent French film from 1928 that tells the story of the martyrdom of Joan of Arc, a young woman who is tried and executed for heresy.

201) Dersu Uzala

Dersu Uzala is a 1975 Soviet-Japanese co-production that tells the story of a nomadic hunter and his friendship with a Russian explorer in the Siberian wilderness.

202) Swades

Swades is a Bollywood drama about an Indian man who returns to his rural village to find his childhood nanny and reconnect with his roots.

203) The Wages of Fear

The Wages of Fear is a classic suspenseful film about a group of desperate men hired to transport dangerous nitroglycerin through treacherous South American terrain.

204) Sherlock Jr.

Sherlock Jr. is a silent comedy film about a projectionist who dreams of becoming a detective and solves a mystery in the dream world.

205) My Father and My Son

My Father and My Son is a drama about a father and son struggling to come to terms with their complicated relationship amidst the political turmoil of 1980s Turkey.

206) Vikram Vedha

Vikram Vedha is an Indian action thriller film about a relentless cop and a criminal on the run, who engage in a game of cat and mouse.

207) Uri: The Surgical Strike

A Bollywood film that depicts the Indian Army's retaliation to a terrorist attack through a covert military operation.

208) Umberto D.

Umberto D. is a poignant Italian neorealist drama about an elderly pensioner struggling to survive in post-war Rome.

209) Bhaag Milkha Bhaag

Bhaag Milkha Bhaag is a biographical sports drama about the life of an Indian athlete, Milkha Singh, and his journey from a troubled past to becoming a world champion runner.

210) Paan Singh Tomar

Paan Singh Tomar is a biographical drama about an Indian athlete who turns to a life of crime after being forced to give up his dreams.

211) Prisoners

A crime-drama film about a father who takes matters into his own hands after his daughter and her friend are kidnapped and the police are unable to find them.

212) The Grand Budapest Hotel

The Grand Budapest Hotel is a whimsical, comedic adventure about the friendship between a hotel concierge and a young lobby boy set in the fictional European country of Zubrowka.

213) Gone Girl

Gone Girl is a psychological thriller that follows a man suspected of murdering his wife, who has mysteriously disappeared.

214) Mad Max: Fury Road

Mad Max: Fury Road is an action-packed post-apocalyptic adventure about a group of rebels trying to escape a tyrannical leader.

215) Rocky

"Rocky" is a movie about a small-time boxer who gets a shot at the heavyweight championship and transforms himself from a struggling fighter to an inspiration.

216) Hacksaw Ridge

Hacksaw Ridge is a 2016 biographical war film about a conscientious objector who served as a medic during World War II and was awarded the Medal of Honor for saving 75 soldiers without carrying a weapon

217) Three Billboards Outside Ebbing, Missouri

Three Billboards Outside Ebbing, Missouri is a dark comedy-drama film about a mother seeking justice for her daughter's murder by renting three billboards to call out the police's lack of progress on the case, leading to a chain of events that brings the town's simmering racial tensions to the surface.

218) Harry Potter and the Deathly Hallows: Part 2

The final installment in the Harry Potter franchise follows Harry and his friends as they battle Lord Voldemort for the fate of the wizarding world.

219) Pirates of the Caribbean: The Curse of the Black Pearl

Pirates of the Caribbean: The Curse of the Black Pearl is an action-packed swashbuckling adventure about a cursed pirate ship, its crew of undead sailors, and the brave heroes who must break the curse.

220) Blade Runner

Blade Runner is a sci-fi neo-noir film about a blade runner tasked with hunting down and retiring a group of rogue replicants who have illegally returned to Earth.

221) Logan

Logan is a dark, intense, and emotional journey of an aging Wolverine who must protect a young mutant girl from a powerful, mysterious enemy.

222) Ford v Ferrari

Ford v Ferrari is a thrilling drama about the rivalry between Ford and Ferrari in the 1966 24 Hours of Le Mans race.

223) The Handmaiden

The Handmaiden is a psychological thriller about a con-artist's plot to defraud a Japanese heiress, which is complicated by the growing romance between the two women involved.

224) Stand by Me

Stand by Me is a coming of age story about four friends who embark on a journey to find the body of a missing boy.

225) The Big Lebowski

The Big Lebowski is a comedic crime-drama about an eccentric, unemployed slacker who gets caught up in a quirky, convoluted kidnapping plot.

226) The Terminator

The Terminator is a science fiction action film about a cyborg assassin from the future sent to kill a woman whose unborn son will one day lead humanity in a war against machines.

227) Catch Me If You Can

Catch Me If You Can follows the story of Frank Abagnale Jr., a young con artist who successfully impersonates an airline pilot, doctor, and lawyer while being pursued by an FBI agent.

228) The Sound of Music

The Sound of Music is a classic musical about a young woman who leaves a convent to become the governess of a large Austrian family and ultimately finds love and acceptance in her new life.

229) Trainspotting

Trainspotting is a darkly comedic drama about a group of young heroin addicts living in Edinburgh, Scotland.

230) Ratatouille

Ratatouille is a heartwarming tale of a rat who dreams of becoming a great chef and overcoming all odds to make his dream come true.

231) Jaws

Jaws is a classic thriller about a great white shark that terrorizes a small beach town.

232) The Help

The Help is a powerful drama about a group of courageous African-American women who risk their jobs and safety to help a young white woman write a book exposing the racism they face in the segregated South.

233) Fargo

Fargo is a darkly comic crime drama about a car salesman's scheme to get rich quick that goes terribly wrong.

234) Dead Poets Society

Dead Poets Society is a 1989 drama film about an English teacher who inspires his students to look at life from a different perspective.

235) The Exorcist

The Exorcist is a horror film about a priest who must battle a demonic presence to save a young girl possessed by a powerful force.

236) Spotlight

Spotlight is a drama about a team of investigative journalists uncovering a scandal of child sexual abuse within the Catholic Church.

237) The Wizard of Oz

The Wizard of Oz is a classic musical fantasy film about a young girl's journey to the magical Land of Oz in search of a way to get home.

238) Before Sunrise

Before Sunrise is a romantic drama about two strangers who meet on a train and spend one night together in Vienna, exploring the city and forming a deep connection.

239) The Deer Hunter

The Deer Hunter is a powerful exploration of the effects of the Vietnam War on a group of friends from a small steel town in Pennsylvania.

240) Into the Wild

Into the Wild follows the journey of Christopher McCandless, a young man who abandons his possessions and hitchhikes to Alaska in search of a deeper understanding of life.

241) Room

Room is a powerful and emotionally-charged story about a mother and her son's resilience in the face of an unimaginable situation.

242) Memories of Murder

Memories of Murder is a South Korean crime-thriller film which follows two detectives as they try to solve a series of unsolved serial murders in a small rural town.

243) Groundhog Day

Groundhog Day follows the story of Phil Connors, a cynical weatherman, as he is forced to relive the same day over and over until he learns to become a better person.

244) 12 Years a Slave

12 Years a Slave is a powerful, emotionally-charged drama about a free African-American man who is kidnapped and sold into slavery in the pre-Civil War United States.

245) Portrait of a Lady on Fire

Portrait of a Lady on Fire is a romance drama about a forbidden relationship between an artist and her subject, set against the backdrop of 18th century France.

246) Platoon

Platoon is a war drama film about a young soldier's journey through the Vietnam War, as he is caught between the two sides of a conflict within his own squad.

247) Monsters, Inc.

Monsters, Inc. is an animated fantasy-comedy film about the monsters of Monstropolis who power their city by harvesting the screams of children, and the unlikely friendship between a monster and a little girl who accidentally enter their world.

248) Hachi: A Dog's Tale

Hachi: A Dog's Tale is a heartwarming story about the unbreakable bond between a dog and his master, and the loyalty and devotion that follows.

249) How to Train Your Dragon

How to Train Your Dragon is an animated adventure about a young Viking who befriends a dragon and learns to appreciate their differences.

250) All Quiet on the Western Front

All Quiet on the Western Front is a powerful anti-war film that follows a group of German soldiers as they experience the horrors of World War I.

251) Rush

Rush is a thrilling biopic about the intense rivalry between two Formula One racers in the 1970s.

252) Gran Torino

Gran Torino is a drama-comedy about an aging Korean War veteran who forms an unlikely bond with his Hmong neighbors as he comes to terms with his past.

253) Million Dollar Baby

Million Dollar Baby is a heart-wrenching drama about an unlikely boxer and her trainer who fight for her dreams of becoming a champion despite the odds.

254) In the Mood for Love

In the Mood for Love is a romantic drama about two people who form an unlikely bond as they try to resist their growing feelings for one another.

255) Stalker

Stalker is a 1979 Russian science fiction psychological drama film that follows a mysterious guide who leads two men into the Zone, an area in which the laws of nature are distorted.

256) My Neighbor Totoro

My Neighbor Totoro is a heartwarming and magical animated film about two young sisters who befriend a magical forest spirit.

257) Wild Tales

Wild Tales is a dark comedy anthology film that follows six stories of revenge, justice, and retribution.

258) Before Sunset

Before Sunset is a romantic drama about two former lovers who reunite in Paris nine years after their initial meeting and explore the possibility of a second chance at love.

259) Barry Lyndon

Barry Lyndon is a period drama following the story of an ambitious man who attempts to rise to the top of the social ladder, but ultimately finds himself in a downward spiral of misfortune.

260) The Iron Giant

The Iron Giant is an animated science fiction film about a young boy who befriends a giant robotic alien and defends his town from an impending government threat.

261) The Red Shoes

The Red Shoes is a classic British drama film about a young ballerina who must choose between her career and her love life.

262) La haine

La haine is a French drama film that follows three young friends from the impoverished suburbs of Paris as they struggle with racism, poverty, and violence.

263) Amores Perros

Amores Perros is a Mexican drama film that follows three interweaving stories of people whose lives are drastically changed by a car accident.

264) Paris, Texas

Paris, Texas is a moving drama about a father and son reconnecting after years of separation.

265) Ben-Hur

Ben-Hur is an epic historical drama about a Jewish prince who seeks revenge against a childhood friend who betrayed him and is ultimately redeemed by Jesus Christ.

266) The Seventh Seal

The Seventh Seal is a classic Swedish film about a knight's existential struggle with death as he plays a game of chess.

267) The Man Who Shot Liberty Valance

The Man Who Shot Liberty Valance is a classic western about a senator who is helped to success by a mysterious gunslinger, only for his past to come back to haunt him.

268) A Silent Voice: The Movie

A Silent Voice: The Movie is a heart-wrenching story about a young boy's journey to redemption after bullying a deaf girl in elementary school.

269) Persona

Persona is a psychological drama about an actress and nurse who switch roles and explore their identities through a series of conversations.

270) Cool Hand Luke

Cool Hand Luke is a classic prison drama about a non-conformist rebel who refuses to conform to the oppressive rules of a Southern chain gang.

271) White Heat

White Heat is a classic crime drama about a psychopathic gangster who is determined to stay on top, no matter the cost.

272) In the Name of the Father

In the Name of the Father tells the story of an innocent man's struggle for justice in the face of wrongful imprisonment for a crime he did not commit.

273) The Third Man

The Third Man is a classic British film noir from 1949, starring Orson Welles as a mysterious criminal in post-World War II Vienna.

274) Network

Network is a satirical film about a news anchor who rebels against his network and calls for viewers to rise up against the injustices of the world.

275) Hotel Rwanda

Hotel Rwanda is a powerful drama that tells the true story of Paul Rusesabagina's heroic efforts to protect his family and hundreds of refugees during the Rwandan genocide of 1994.

276) On the Waterfront

On the Waterfront follows a former boxer's struggle to stand up to the mob-controlled union of the waterfront and fight for justice.

277) Rebecca

Rebecca is a Gothic romance thriller about a young woman who is haunted by the memory of her husband's dead first wife.

278) Paper Moon

Paper Moon is a charming comedy-drama about a con-artist and a young orphan girl who team up to scam their way across the American Midwest during the Great Depression.

279) The Celebration

The Celebration is a 1998 Danish drama film that follows a family reunion that quickly spirals out of control as secrets are revealed and old wounds are reopened.

280) Mary and Max

Mary and Max is a heartwarming stop-motion animation film about the unlikely friendship between an 8-year-old girl from Australia and a 44-year-old man with Asperger's Syndrome from New York.

281) The Best Years of Our Lives

The Best Years of Our Lives is a classic post-WWII drama that follows the struggles of three veterans as they attempt to reintegrate into civilian life.

282) The Grapes of Wrath

The Grapes of Wrath is a classic American drama about a family of Oklahoma farmers forced to migrate to California during the Dust Bowl of the 1930s.

283) It Happened One Night

It Happened One Night is a romantic comedy about a spoiled heiress and a newspaper reporter who fall in love while traveling cross-country.

284) Three Colors: Red

Three Colors: Red is a 1994 French drama film about a retired judge who investigates the relationships between two strangers and discovers the power of human connection.

285) PK

PK is a satirical comedy-drama about an alien who comes to Earth and experiences the complexities of human life, religion, and relationships.

286) Fanny and Alexander

Fanny and Alexander is a story of two siblings coming of age in a family of strong personalities, exploring the joys and sorrows of life.

287) The 400 Blows

The 400 Blows is an acclaimed French New Wave drama about a young boy's struggles with society and his tumultuous home life.

288) Wild Strawberries

Wild Strawberries is a classic Swedish drama about an elderly professor who embarks on a journey of self-discovery and reflection.

289) A Woman Under the Influence

A Woman Under the Influence is a powerful drama about a woman struggling with mental illness and the effect it has on her family.

290) Mr. Smith Goes to Washington

Mr. Smith Goes to Washington is a classic American political drama about an idealistic small-town senator who takes on the corrupt political establishment in Washington, D.C.

291) Andrei Rublev

Andrei Rublev is a biographical drama about the life of a 15th-century Russian icon painter, exploring the artist's struggles with his faith, his art, and the world around him.

292) Underground

Underground is a 1995 historical drama set in Yugoslavia during World War II, following two resistance fighters who risk their lives to save a group of people from Nazi persecution.

293) The Message

The Message is an epic historical drama about the life of the Prophet Muhammad and the birth of the Islamic faith.

294) Inherit the Wind

Inherit the Wind is a film about a small town's struggle with the clash between science and religion in the 1920s.

295) The General

The General is a classic silent comedy film about a train engineer who goes to great lengths to rescue his beloved locomotive from the Union army during the American Civil War.

296) Farewell My Concubine

Farewell My Concubine is a tragic story of two performers in the Beijing Opera who are bound by a lifelong friendship and their struggles to survive during a tumultuous time in Chinese history.

297) Sunrise

Sunrise is a silent romantic drama about a married man who is tempted away from his wife by a vamp from the city.

298) Lagaan: Once Upon a Time in India

Lagaan: Once Upon a Time in India is a Bollywood musical drama about a small village in India that must win a cricket match against the British in order to be freed from oppressive taxation.

299) The Battle of Algiers

The Battle of Algiers is a 1965 war drama film depicting the events of the Algerian War of Independence from the French colonial rule in the 1950s.

300) Winter Sleep

Winter Sleep is a Turkish drama about a wealthy landlord's struggle to come to terms with his life and relationships in a small Anatolian village.

301) Wolf Children

Wolf Children is a heartwarming story about a single mother raising two children who are part-wolf and her struggles to keep them safe and help them find their place in the world.

302) Diabolique

Diabolique is a suspenseful psychological thriller about two women who conspire to murder the cruel headmaster of a private school, only to find that their scheme has unexpected and deadly consequences.

303) The Hidden Fortress

The Hidden Fortress is an action-adventure samurai film about two peasants who accompany a princess and a general on a dangerous mission to recover her family's lost gold.

304) Throne of Blood

Throne of Blood is a 1957 Japanese film adaptation of Shakespeare's Macbeth, set in feudal Japan, in which a samurai's ambition leads to his downfall.

305) The Gold Rush

The Gold Rush is a classic silent comedy about a prospector who embarks on a quest to find gold in the frozen Klondike, encountering a variety of characters and obstacles along the way.

306) Autumn Sonata

Autumn Sonata tells the story of a strained mother-daughter relationship that is tested when they reunite after many years of estrangement.

307) Time of the Gypsies

Time of the Gypsies is a magical realist drama about a young Romani man's coming of age and his journey to find his place in the world.

308) Ace in the Hole

Ace in the Hole is a film about a cynical journalist who exploits a tragedy for personal gain.

309) Barfi!

Barfi! is a heartwarming romantic comedy about a deaf-mute man's quest for true love in a big city.

310) Munna Bhai M.B.B.S.

Munna Bhai M.B.B.S. is a comedy-drama about an underworld don who pretends to be a doctor to fulfill his father's wish.

311) Raise the Red Lantern

Raise the Red Lantern is a drama about a young woman's struggle to survive in a turbulent and oppressive environment as the fourth wife of a wealthy Chinese warlord.

312) Rang De Basanti

Rang De Basanti is a story of a group of young Indians who, inspired by the revolutionary spirit of their ancestors, take a stand against the corrupt system.

313) The Virgin Spring

The Virgin Spring is a 1960 Swedish drama film about a pious Christian girl who is brutally raped and murdered, and her father's struggle with his desire for revenge.

314) Dil Chahta Hai

Dil Chahta Hai is a coming-of-age story about three close friends who go through different life experiences and learn about the importance of friendship and relationships.

315) Nights of Cabiria

Nights of Cabiria is a 1957 Italian neorealist drama film directed by Federico Fellini, which follows the life of a prostitute in Rome who searches for true love and happiness.

316) Tangerines

Tangerines is a powerful drama about two Estonian farmers who form an unlikely bond while caring for wounded soldiers during the 1992 conflict in the former Soviet Republic of Abkhazia.

317) Rififi

Rififi is a classic French heist film that follows a group of criminals as they plan and execute an intricate jewelry store robbery.

318) Bajrangi Bhaijaan

Bajrangi Bhaijaan is a heartwarming story of an unlikely bond between a mute Pakistani girl and a devoted Indian man who embarks on a journey to reunite her with her family.

319) Pink

Pink is a compelling courtroom drama that explores the complexities of consent and gender roles in India.

320) Article 15

Article 15 is a gripping crime drama that follows a police officer as he investigates a horrific crime against a marginalized group in rural India.

321) Talvar

Talvar is a gripping crime-drama that follows the investigation of a double-murder case in Delhi, India, and the subsequent trial that ensues.

322) Jean de Florette

Jean de Florette is a story of a man's struggle to realize his dream of owning a farm, in spite of the machinations of his greedy neighbors.

323) Queen

Queen is a biographical drama about the life of Indian actress and politician, Jayalalithaa Jayaram, and her rise to power.

324) The Grand Illusion

The Grand Illusion is a 1937 French war drama film that follows a group of French officers as they attempt to escape a German POW camp during World War I.

325) Sholay

Sholay is an Indian action-adventure film about two ex-convicts who are hired to protect a small village from a notorious bandit.

326) OMG: Oh My God!

OMG: Oh My God! is a satirical comedy-drama about a man who takes God to court after his shop is destroyed by an earthquake.

327) A Wednesday

A Wednesday is a thrilling cat-and-mouse game between a mysterious caller and a police commissioner as they attempt to prevent a series of bombings in Mumbai.

328) The Bandit

The Bandit is a comedy-drama about a down-on-his-luck truck driver who embarks on a cross-country journey to deliver a mysterious package and win the heart of a beautiful woman.

329) The Circus

The Circus is a classic silent film comedy about a tramp who finds himself in a chaotic circus, full of misadventures and hilarity.

330) Let's Go! India

Let's Go! India is a comedy-drama about a young Indian couple who embark on a road trip to explore their country, discovering new places and experiences along the way.

331) Kahaani

Kahaani is a thrilling mystery drama about a pregnant woman's search for her missing husband in the bustling city of Kolkata.

332) Masaan

Masaan is a powerful drama about two young people in Varanasi, India struggling to overcome the social and cultural pressures of their environment.

333) Hera Pheri

Hera Pheri is a classic Bollywood comedy about three unemployed men who get caught up in a series of chaotic and hilarious situations as they try to make some quick money.

334) Black

Black is a powerful and emotional drama about a blind and deaf girl who learns to cope with her disabilities and find her place in the world.

335) Udaan

Udaan is a coming-of-age drama that follows a teenage boy's struggles to break free from the oppressive control of his father and pursue his dreams.

336) Her Sey Çok Güzel Olacak

Her Sey Çok Güzel Olacak is a romantic comedy about a woman who learns to embrace life and love despite the challenges she faces.

337) Anand

Anand is a heartwarming and uplifting story about friendship and the power of optimism in the face of adversity.

338) Sarfarosh

Sarfarosh is a thrilling Indian action drama about a police officer's mission to take down a terrorist organization and protect the country from their threats.

339) Everything Everywhere All at Once

Everything Everywhere All at Once is a heartwarming documentary about a group of high school students who embark on an inspiring journey to explore their passions and discover their purpose.

340) Dune

Dune is a sci-fi epic set in a distant future where a young nobleman must lead a nomadic tribe to save his home planet from a powerful emperor.

341) Blade Runner 2049

Blade Runner 2049 is a sci-fi neo-noir sequel to the 1982 classic, set thirty years later, which follows a new Blade Runner as he uncovers a dark secret that could plunge what's left of society into chaos.

342) Black Swan

Black Swan follows a ballet dancer's journey of self-discovery as she struggles with her own dark side while preparing for the lead role in Swan Lake.

343) La La Land

La La Land is a romantic musical comedy-drama about two aspiring artists who fall in love while pursuing their dreams in Los Angeles.

344) Her

Her is a romantic science-fiction drama about a man who falls in love with an advanced computer operating system.

345) CODA

CODA is a heartwarming coming-of-age story about a deaf teenager who must choose between following her dreams of pursuing a career in music or staying home to help her family run their struggling fishing business.

346) Guardians of the Galaxy

Guardians of the Galaxy is a thrilling sci-fi adventure about a group of misfits who must save the universe from a powerful villain.

347) The Princess Bride

The Princess Bride is a classic romantic adventure comedy about true love conquering all obstacles.

348) Donnie Darko

Donnie Darko is a psychological thriller about a troubled teenager who is visited by a mysterious figure and begins to unravel a sinister time-travel conspiracy.

349) Zack Snyder's Justice League

Zack Snyder's Justice League is a four-hour-long superhero epic that follows the formation of a team of DC Comics' greatest heroes as they battle to save the world from the alien forces of Steppenwolf.

350) Sin City

Sin City is a neo-noir crime thriller film based on Frank Miller's graphic novel series, featuring a cast of criminals, corrupt politicians, and desperate individuals struggling to survive in a corrupt city.

351) The Revenant

The Revenant is a survival story of a fur trapper who seeks revenge on the men who left him for dead after a bear attack.

352) Deadpool

Deadpool is an irreverent and hilarious action-packed superhero movie about an antihero with superhuman abilities and a dark sense of humor.

353) The Avengers

The Avengers is a superhero action-adventure film about a team of superheroes coming together to save the world from an alien invasion.

354) Casino Royale

Casino Royale is a thrilling spy movie that follows James Bond as he takes on a dangerous mission to stop a criminal organization from taking control of a high-stakes poker game.

355) JFK

JFK is a political thriller that follows the investigation into the assassination of President John F. Kennedy.

356) The Martian

The Martian is a science fiction drama about an astronaut who is stranded on Mars and must use his ingenuity and resourcefulness to survive and find a way back to Earth.

357) Zootopia

Zootopia is an animated comedy-adventure about a rookie bunny cop who teams up with a con artist fox to uncover a conspiracy that threatens the city of Zootopia.

358) The Imitation Game

The Imitation Game is a biographical drama about Alan Turing, a brilliant mathematician and cryptanalyst who helps the Allies win WW2 by breaking the Nazi's Enigma code.

359) Dances with Wolves

Dances with Wolves is a western drama about a Civil War soldier who befriends a tribe of Native Americans and learns to appreciate their culture and way of life.

360) Lion

Lion is a heartwarming drama about an Indian boy's journey to find his lost family after being separated from them as a child.

361) The Incredibles

The Incredibles is a super-powered family comedy-adventure about a family of undercover superheroes who must save the world while balancing their family life.

362) Beauty and the Beast

Beauty and the Beast is a classic Disney animated musical about a young woman who falls in love with a cursed prince who takes the form of a beast.

363) The Invisible Guest

The Invisible Guest is a Spanish thriller about a businessman who must prove his innocence in a mysterious murder case.

364) Soul

Soul follows the journey of a jazz musician who discovers the true meaning of life after a near-death experience.

365) The Pursuit of Happyness

The Pursuit of Happyness is a heartwarming story about a father's determination to provide a better life for his son despite his own financial struggles.

366) Magnolia

Magnolia is a complex and emotionally charged exploration of the interconnected lives of several characters in Los Angeles.

367) Aladdin

Aladdin is a classic Disney animated musical comedy-adventure about a street urchin who uses a magical genie to win the heart of a beautiful princess.

368) 12 Monkeys

12 Monkeys is a sci-fi thriller about a time traveler sent from the future to prevent a deadly virus from wiping out humanity.

369) Slumdog Millionaire

Slumdog Millionaire is a heartwarming story of a young man from the slums of Mumbai who, against all odds, goes on to win the top prize on a popular Indian game show.

370) Rain Man

Rain Man tells the story of an estranged brotherhood between a self-centered young man and his autistic savant older brother, as they embark on a cross-country journey of discovery and redemption.

371) Perfect Blue

Perfect Blue is a psychological thriller about a former pop star's struggle to adapt to her new life as an actress, and the terrifying consequences that ensue.

372) The Graduate

The Graduate follows a recent college graduate as he struggles to find his place in the world and ultimately discovers the importance of self-fulfillment.

373) Big Fish

Big Fish is a fantastical journey of a father and son's relationship, in which the father recounts his life's adventures that may or may not be true.

374) Blood Diamond

Blood Diamond is a thrilling drama that follows a mercenary, a smuggler, and a fisherman as they search for a valuable gem in a war-torn African country.

375) Scent of a Woman

Scent of a Woman is a drama about a retired Army officer who takes a young student on a journey of self-discovery while teaching him about life, love, and courage.

376) The King's Speech

The King's Speech is a biographical drama about King George VI of England and his struggle to overcome a speech impediment with the help of an unconventional speech therapist.

377) Kill Bill: Vol. 2

Kill Bill: Vol. 2 follows the Bride's quest for revenge against her former allies as she continues her journey for justice.

378) Rosemary's Baby

Rosemary's Baby is a psychological horror film about a young couple who move into a new apartment, only to find that their unborn child may be the target of a sinister cult.

379) Young Frankenstein

Young Frankenstein is a classic horror comedy about a scientist who attempts to create a monster from the remains of his grandfather's experiments.

380) Planet of the Apes

Planet of the Apes is a science fiction classic that follows a group of astronauts who crash-land on a strange planet inhabited by intelligent, talking apes.

381) Butch Cassidy and the Sundance Kid

Butch Cassidy and the Sundance Kid is a classic Western about two outlaws on the run from a relentless posse.

382) Baahubali: The Beginning

Baahubali: The Beginning is an epic Indian action-adventure film about the battle between two brothers for the throne of an ancient kingdom.

383) Akira

Akira is a classic anime sci-fi action film about a secret government project and two teenage friends caught in a battle that threatens to destroy Neo-Tokyo.

384) Dog Day Afternoon

Dog Day Afternoon is a 1975 crime drama film about a man who attempts to rob a bank to pay for his lover's sex reassignment surgery, and the ensuing hostage crisis.

385) Fiddler on the Roof

Fiddler on the Roof is a musical comedy-drama about a Jewish family living in the Pale of Settlement of Imperial Russia in the early 20th century, struggling to maintain their religious and cultural traditions while facing anti-semitism and changing social mores.

386) Dogville

Dogville is a dark drama about a small town in America that takes in a mysterious woman, only to discover that the price of her stay is much higher than they expected.

387) Life of Brian

Life of Brian is a Monty Python comedy about a man mistaken for a messiah who must navigate the challenges of life in ancient Judea.

388) Chungking Express

Chungking Express is a romantic comedy-drama about two lovelorn cops in Hong Kong and the women who enter their lives.

389) High Noon

High Noon is a classic western about a small-town marshal who must face a gang of deadly killers alone.

390) The Bourne Ultimatum

The Bourne Ultimatum is a thrilling action movie about Jason Bourne's quest to uncover his true identity and avenge the death of his lover.

391) Sling Blade

Sling Blade is a drama about a mentally challenged man who is released from a psychiatric hospital and struggles to find his place in the world.

392) 8½

8½ is a surrealist exploration of a director's creative block and his inner struggles with his personal and professional life.

393) Annie Hall

Annie Hall is a romantic comedy about the relationship between neurotic comedian Alvy Singer and the free-spirited Annie Hall.

394) Rio Bravo

Rio Bravo is a classic western about a sheriff, his deputy, and their ragtag group of friends who must protect a small town from a powerful outlaw.

395) Roman Holiday

Roman Holiday is a romantic comedy about a princess on a secret journey of self-discovery in Rome.

396) The Hustler

The Hustler follows the story of an ambitious pool hustler as he attempts to become the best in the world while struggling with personal demons.

397) Gandhi

Gandhi is a biographical drama about the life of Mahatma Gandhi, who led India to independence through his philosophy of non-violent civil disobedience.

398) The Last Picture Show

The Last Picture Show is a coming-of-age drama about two Texas teenagers navigating the complexities of growing up in a small town in the 1950s.

399) Papillon

Papillon is a powerful biographical drama about a man's fight for freedom and survival while unjustly imprisoned on a remote island penal colony.

400) Infernal Affairs

Infernal Affairs is a Hong Kong crime thriller about an undercover cop and a mole in the police force who are unknowingly working for the same target.

401) Solaris

Solaris is a sci-fi drama about a psychologist sent to a space station orbiting a mysterious planet to investigate the crew's strange behavior.

402) The Maltese Falcon

The Maltese Falcon is a classic film noir about a private detective's search for a priceless statuette and the dangerous people who are after it.

403) Quo Vadis, Aida?

Quo Vadis, Aida is a powerful drama about a Bosnian translator working for the UN who is forced to choose between her family and her duty to protect her people during the 1995 Srebrenica genocide.

404) Ip Man

Ip Man is a biographical martial arts film about the life of the legendary Wing Chun master, Ip Man, and his struggles in the city of Foshan during the Sino-Japanese War.

405) Being There

Being There is a comedic drama about a simple-minded gardener who is mistaken for a wise and powerful advisor after a series of chance encounters.

406) La Dolce Vita

La Dolce Vita is a 1960 Italian drama film that follows the life of a journalist as he searches for the meaning of life amidst the hedonistic lifestyle of Rome's elite.

407) The Night of the Hunter

The Night of the Hunter is a classic thriller about a sinister preacher who goes on a hunt for two young children who possess the secret to a hidden fortune.

408) Pink Floyd: The Wall

Pink Floyd: The Wall is a surrealistic musical drama about a rock star's mental breakdown and subsequent journey of self-discovery.

409) Cinderella Man

Cinderella Man is a biographical sports drama film about the life of boxer James J. Braddock, who rises from a poverty-stricken life to become a world heavyweight champion.

410) Mommy

Mommy is a heart-wrenching drama about a single mother struggling to raise her troubled teenage son.

411) What Ever Happened to Baby Jane?

What Ever Happened to Baby Jane? is a psychological thriller about two aging sisters, Baby Jane and Blanche, who are locked in a bitter rivalry that leads to a shocking climax.

412) Castle in the Sky

Castle in the Sky is an animated adventure film about two children searching for a legendary floating castle while being pursued by a sinister army.

413) Nausicaä of the Valley of the Wind

Nausicaä of the Valley of the Wind is an animated post-apocalyptic fantasy adventure about a young princess who must save her kingdom from an impending disaster.

414) Wings of Desire

Wings of Desire is a poetic and dreamlike exploration of the lives of angels in Berlin, as they observe the struggles and joys of the human condition.

415) Neon Genesis Evangelion: The End of Evangelion

Neon Genesis Evangelion: The End of Evangelion is an apocalyptic psychological action drama that follows the story of the human race's final battle against the Angels as the fate of humanity hangs in the balance.

416) The Straight Story

The Straight Story is a heartwarming drama about an elderly man's journey to reconcile with his estranged brother.

417) Wolfwalkers

Wolfwalkers is an animated fantasy adventure about a young apprentice hunter who befriends a wild native girl who can transform into a wolf.

418) Anatomy of a Murder

Anatomy of a Murder is a courtroom drama that follows a murder trial, exploring the motivations of the accused and the impact of the crime on the victim's family.

419) The Cabinet of Dr. Caligari

The Cabinet of Dr. Caligari is a 1920 German Expressionist horror film about a sinister hypnotist who uses a somnambulist to commit murders.

420) Who's Afraid of Virginia Woolf?

Who's Afraid of Virginia Woolf? is a dark psychological drama about an aging couple's volatile and destructive marriage.

421) Elite Squad

Elite Squad is an intense and gritty crime drama that follows two police officers as they attempt to take down a powerful drug cartel in Rio de Janeiro.

422) Mirror

Mirror is a surreal psychological horror film about a man who begins to experience supernatural events after being visited by a mysterious woman.

423) Touch of Evil

Touch of Evil is a classic crime noir film about a corrupt lawman and a Mexican couple who become embroiled in a murder investigation.

424) The Leopard

The Leopard is a sweeping epic about a Sicilian nobleman's attempts to maintain his family's status amidst the sweeping changes of the Italian Risorgimento.

425) Secrets & Lies

Secrets & Lies is a British drama film about a woman who discovers her birth mother and the dramatic consequences that follow.

426) The Legend of 1900

The Legend of 1900 is a story about a talented pianist who is born and raised on a transatlantic ocean liner, and never sets foot on land.

427) Nobody Knows

Nobody Knows is a Japanese drama film about a family of four children living in Tokyo, abandoned by their mother and left to fend for themselves.

428) Goodbye, Children

Goodbye, Children is a French drama about a group of Jewish students in a Catholic boarding school during World War II who must confront the harsh realities of the Holocaust.

429) The Killing

The Killing is a classic film noir that follows a racetrack heist gone wrong and the aftermath of the crime.

430) Le Samouraï

Le Samouraï is a French crime film that follows the story of a hitman who is trying to find out who is trying to frame him for a murder he didn't commit.

431) Fitzcarraldo

Fitzcarraldo is a story of one man's obsession to build an opera house in the Amazon rainforest and the extreme lengths he goes to in order to achieve his dream.

432) The Diving Bell and the Butterfly

The Diving Bell and the Butterfly is a powerful and inspiring story of a man who is paralyzed, yet finds a way to communicate and live life to the fullest.

433) The Tale of The Princess Kaguya

The Tale of The Princess Kaguya is an animated fantasy film about a magical princess who is found inside a bamboo stalk and must choose between staying with her adoptive family or returning to her true home in the moon.

434) Song of the Sea

Song of the Sea is an animated fantasy film about a young boy who discovers he is a selkie, a mythical creature that can transform from a human to a seal, and embarks on a quest to save his family and the spirit world.

435) Dilwale Dulhania Le Jayenge

Dilwale Dulhania Le Jayenge is a classic Bollywood romantic comedy about two young people who must overcome family and cultural obstacles to be together.

436) Stalag 17

Stalag 17 is a classic World War II comedy-drama about a group of Allied prisoners of war trying to escape a German POW camp.

437) My Sassy Girl

My Sassy Girl is a romantic comedy about a college student who falls in love with a mysterious girl who has a wild and unpredictable personality.

438) La strada

La Strada is a heartbreaking story of a young girl's journey of self-discovery, set against a backdrop of poverty and tragedy.

439) Out of the Past

Out of the Past is a classic film noir about a former private detective who is forced to confront his dark past when an old flame resurfaces.

440) Persepolis

Persepolis is an autobiographical animated film about a young girl's coming-of-age story during the Iranian Revolution.

441) Nostalghia

Nostalghia is a poetic and philosophical exploration of longing, isolation, and the human spirit in a remote and desolate part of Italy.

442) Brief Encounter

Brief Encounter is a 1945 British romantic drama about two strangers who meet and fall in love, but ultimately decide to remain loyal to their respective spouses.

443) The Sea Inside

The Sea Inside is a drama about the struggle of a man to win the right to end his own life with dignity.

444) The Shop Around the Corner

The Shop Around the Corner is a romantic comedy about two feuding coworkers who unknowingly fall in love with each other through anonymous letters.

445) Sleuth

Sleuth is a psychological thriller involving a game of cat and mouse between a wealthy writer and his wife's lover.

446) Cries & Whispers

Cries & Whispers is a powerful drama about three sisters struggling to cope with the death of their mother and the secrets and pain that are revealed as they come together to say goodbye.

447) Black Cat, White Cat

Black Cat, White Cat is a comedic Balkan crime caper that follows the chaotic adventures of two feuding gypsy families.

448) Spring, Summer, Fall, Winter... and Spring

Spring, Summer, Fall, Winter... and Spring is a poetic story of a Buddhist monk's life journey and spiritual growth over the course of five seasons.

449) Sweet Smell of Success

Sweet Smell of Success is a dark and cynical drama that follows the ruthless machinations of a powerful New York City gossip columnist.

450) Departures

Departures is a Japanese drama about a young man who finds purpose and acceptance in his life by taking a job as an undertaker.

451) The Exterminating Angel

The Exterminating Angel is a surrealist film about a group of upper-class people who are mysteriously unable to leave a dinner party.

452) Ivan's Childhood

Ivan's Childhood tells the story of a young boy's struggle to survive in the midst of World War II.

453) Elite Squad 2: The Enemy Within

Elite Squad 2: The Enemy Within is a thrilling crime drama that follows the elite Brazilian police unit BOPE as they battle corruption and organized crime in Rio de Janeiro.

454) G.O.R.A.

G.O.R.A. is a sci-fi adventure comedy about a man who is abducted by aliens and must find a way to get back home.

455) Haider

Haider is a tragedy about a young man's search for justice and revenge in a war-torn Kashmir.

456) Kind Hearts and Coronets

Kind Hearts and Coronets is a darkly comedic British film about a man who seeks revenge on the aristocratic family who denied him his inheritance by systematically assassinating each of his relatives in order to claim the title for himself.

457) Through a Glass Darkly

Through a Glass Darkly is a psychological drama about a family whose relationships unravel as they confront the demons of mental illness and the limits of faith.

458) Central Station

Central Station is a poignant Brazilian drama about an old woman and a young boy who form an unlikely friendship as they embark on a journey to find the boy's father.

459) Rome, Open City

Rome, Open City is a 1945 Italian neorealist drama film that follows the struggles of a resistance movement in Nazi-occupied Rome during World War II.

460) Tae Guk Gi: The Brotherhood of War

Tae Guk Gi: The Brotherhood of War is a powerful and emotional drama about two brothers who are forced to fight for their country during the Korean War.

461) Sanjuro

Sanjuro is a classic samurai film about a ronin who helps a group of unsuspecting samurai solve a local dispute.

462) Winter Light

Winter Light is a powerful drama about a pastor's struggle with faith, doubt, and despair in a small Swedish village.

463) Carry On, Munna Bhai

Carry On, Munna Bhai is a comedy-drama about a kind-hearted gangster who tries to win a radio contest to impress a girl while hiding his true identity.

464) Nefes: Vatan Sagolsun

Nefes: Vatan Sagolsun is a Turkish drama that follows a young man's journey to discover his true identity and save his country from a dangerous conspiracy.

465) Vizontele

Vizontele is a comedy-drama about a small village in Turkey in the 1970s and the impact that the arrival of the country's first television has on its inhabitants.

466) Andaz Apna Apna

Andaz Apna Apna is a classic Indian comedy about two slackers who unknowingly become embroiled in a plot to inherit a fortune.

467) Special 26

Special 26 is a Bollywood heist movie about a group of con artists who pose as CBI officers to carry out an elaborate sting operation.

468) Puss in Boots: The Last Wish

Puss in Boots: The Last Wish is an animated adventure film about a brave cat who embarks on a quest to save his village from an evil witch's curse.

469) Knives Out

Knives Out is a murder mystery film that follows a family gathering gone wrong when the patriarch is found dead and a renowned detective must investigate the case.

470) Avatar

Avatar is a sci-fi epic set on the alien planet of Pandora, where a disabled human takes on an alien form to help the Na'vi people save their home from destruction.

471) RRR

RRR is an epic period drama about two freedom fighters who join forces to fight against the oppressive British Raj in 1920s India.

472) Titanic

Titanic is a tragic love story set on a doomed ocean liner in 1912.

473) The Blues Brothers

The Blues Brothers is a musical comedy about two brothers who embark on a mission to save an orphanage from foreclosure by putting their old band back together and performing a benefit concert.

474) In Bruges

In Bruges is a dark comedy about two hitmen hiding out in the Belgian city of Bruges while dealing with the repercussions of a difficult job.

475) Sing Street

Sing Street is a coming-of-age musical comedy-drama about a teenage boy in 1980s Dublin who starts a band to impress a girl and find his place in the world.

476) Bohemian Rhapsody

Bohemian Rhapsody is a biographical drama about the life and career of Queen frontman Freddie Mercury, focusing on the band's formative years leading up to their iconic 1985 Live Aid performance.

477) Harry Potter and the Prisoner of Azkaban

In Harry Potter and the Prisoner of Azkaban, Harry and his friends must face a dangerous escaped prisoner while also learning to control their own magical abilities.

478) Mulholland Drive

Mulholland Drive is a surreal neo-noir mystery film about a woman trying to find her identity in the labyrinth of Hollywood.

479) Shrek

Shrek is an animated comedy about an ogre who embarks on a journey to reclaim his swamp and rescue a princess from a dragon-guarded castle.

480) Arrival

Arrival follows a linguist who is tasked with deciphering an alien language in order to communicate with extraterrestrial visitors and avert an impending global crisis.

481) This Is Spinal Tap

This Is Spinal Tap is a mockumentary that follows the misadventures of the British heavy metal band Spinal Tap as they embark on an ill-fated tour of the United States.

482) True Romance

True Romance is a crime-romance film about a couple who fall in love and go on the run after stealing a large amount of cocaine from the mob.

483) The Perks of Being a Wallflower

The Perks of Being a Wallflower is a coming-of-age story about a shy teenager navigating high school and life's complex social dynamics with the help of his two newfound friends.

484) Jojo Rabbit

Jojo Rabbit is a humorous and heartfelt coming-of-age story about a young German boy during World War II who finds an unlikely ally in his imaginary friend, an idiotic version of Adolf Hitler.

485) Almost Famous

Almost Famous is a coming-of-age comedy-drama about a teenage journalist who goes on tour with a rock band during the 1970s.

486) Boogie Nights

Boogie Nights is a film about a young man's rise and fall in the Golden Age of Porn in the San Fernando Valley.

487) Iron Man

Iron Man is a superhero film about a wealthy industrialist and genius inventor who builds a mechanized suit of armor to fight evil.

488) Edward Scissorhands

Edward Scissorhands is a fantasy romance film about a man with scissors for hands who learns to love and be loved despite his unique condition.

489) Edge of Tomorrow

Edge of Tomorrow is a sci-fi action movie about a soldier who finds himself in a time loop, fighting an alien invasion.

490) Star Trek

Star Trek follows the adventures of the crew of the USS Enterprise as they explore the galaxy, encountering alien civilizations and defending the United Federation of Planets.

491) Thor: Ragnarok

Thor: Ragnarok is a comedic action-adventure film that follows Thor's journey to save Asgard from destruction while also facing off against his long-lost sister, Hela.

492) E.T. the Extra-Terrestrial

E.T. the Extra-Terrestrial is a classic, heartwarming story of a young boy who befriends an alien and helps him find his way home.

493) In the Heat of the Night

In the Heat of the Night is a 1967 crime drama film about a Black police detective from Philadelphia who gets caught up in a murder investigation in a small Southern town.

494) Marriage Story

Marriage Story follows a couple's struggles to maintain their relationship as they navigate the complexities of divorce.

495) Children of Men

Children of Men is a dystopian movie about a world where women have become infertile and a man must protect a miraculously pregnant woman to save humanity.

496) Doctor Zhivago

Doctor Zhivago is a romantic epic that follows the life of a Russian doctor and poet who is torn between his love for two women amidst the turmoil of the Russian Revolution.

497) Crouching Tiger, Hidden Dragon

Crouching Tiger, Hidden Dragon is an epic martial arts fantasy film about two warriors in pursuit of a legendary sword and a mysterious warrior.

498) The Bourne Identity

The Bourne Identity is a thrilling action-adventure movie about an amnesiac secret agent on the run from mysterious assassins while trying to uncover his true identity.

499) Mystic River

Mystic River is a powerful drama about three childhood friends in Boston whose lives are forever changed when one of them is the victim of a violent crime.

500) Wonder

Wonder is a heartwarming story about a young boy with facial differences who bravely navigates the challenges of attending a mainstream school.

501) Fantastic Mr. Fox

Fantastic Mr. Fox is an animated film about a clever fox who outsmarts three mean farmers in order to save his family and friends from starvation.

502) Dallas Buyers Club

Dallas Buyers Club is a biographical drama that follows the story of Ron Woodroof, a man diagnosed with AIDS who smuggles unapproved pharmaceutical drugs into Texas to help himself and other AIDS patients.

503) District 9

District 9 is a science fiction action film about an extraterrestrial race forced to live in slum-like conditions on Earth.

504) Life of Pi

Life of Pi is a thrilling adventure story about a young man's journey of faith and survival on a lifeboat with a Bengal tiger.

505) Shaun of the Dead

Shaun of the Dead is a horror-comedy about a group of misfits fighting off a zombie apocalypse in London.

506) X-Men: Days of Future Past

X-Men: Days of Future Past is a sci-fi action film about a group of mutants who must travel back in time to prevent a catastrophic future.

507) The Wrestler

The Wrestler is a drama about a washed-up professional wrestler trying to make a comeback and reconnect with his estranged daughter.

508) Boyhood

Boyhood is a coming-of-age story that follows a young boy named Mason as he grows up over the course of 12 years.

509) Do the Right Thing

Do the Right Thing is a powerful drama that follows the lives of a diverse community in Brooklyn as they grapple with racial tensions, police brutality, and the meaning of justice.

510) The Nightmare Before Christmas

The Nightmare Before Christmas is a stop-motion animated musical fantasy film about the misadventures of Jack Skellington, the Pumpkin King of Halloween Town, as he attempts to take over Christmas.

511) Carlito's Way

Carlito's Way is a crime drama about a former Puerto Rican drug lord attempting to escape his criminal past and start a new life.

512) Toy Story 2

Toy Story 2 follows the adventures of Woody, Buzz, and the rest of the gang as they work together to rescue Woody from a toy collector.

513) Spartacus

Spartacus is a 1960 historical epic film about a slave-turned-gladiator who leads a rebellious uprising against the Roman Empire.

514) Before Midnight

Before Midnight is a romantic drama that follows a couple's journey of love, growth, and commitment over the course of nine years.

515) Brazil

Brazil is a surreal dark comedy about a daydreamer who gets caught up in a nightmarish bureaucratic system while trying to save the woman he loves.

516) Shoplifters

Shoplifters is a heartwarming drama about a family of small-time criminals who find solace in each other despite their hard lives.

517) Let the Right One In

Let the Right One In is a Swedish horror/romance film about a young boy who befriends a vampire child and must protect her from the dangers of the outside world.

518) The Ten Commandments

The Ten Commandments is a 1956 epic film about the life of Moses and his struggle to free the Hebrews from slavery in Egypt.

519) Blood In, Blood Out

Blood In, Blood Out is a drama about three Mexican-American cousins struggling to survive in East Los Angeles and the consequences of their choices.

520) A Christmas Story

A Christmas Story is a classic holiday comedy about a young boy's quest to get a Red Ryder BB Gun for Christmas.

521) Ghost in the Shell

Ghost in the Shell is a sci-fi action movie about a cyborg policewoman who leads the fight against a powerful hacker called the Puppet Master.

522) Charade

Charade is a classic romantic comedy-mystery starring Cary Grant and Audrey Hepburn, in which a widow is pursued by criminals searching for her late husband's stolen fortune.

523) The Man from Earth

The Man from Earth is a science fiction drama about a professor who reveals to his colleagues that he is actually a 14,000-year-old man.

524) The Raid 2

The Raid 2 follows Rama as he goes undercover to infiltrate a crime syndicate and take them down from the inside.

525) A Fistful of Dollars

A Fistful of Dollars is a classic western about a mysterious stranger who plays two rival families against each other in a town torn apart by greed, corruption, and revenge.

526) Harold and Maude

Harold and Maude is a quirky dark comedy about the unlikely romance between a young man and an elderly woman.

527) The Artist

The Artist is a silent, black-and-white film about a fading silent film star who falls in love with an aspiring young actress.

528) All the President's Men

All the President's Men is a gripping political thriller based on the true story of the Washington Post's investigation into the Watergate scandal that brought down President Richard Nixon.

529) The Searchers

The Searchers follows a Civil War veteran on a five-year quest to find his niece who was kidnapped by Comanche Indians.

530) A Streetcar Named Desire

A Streetcar Named Desire tells the story of a woman's struggle to maintain her fading Southern belle lifestyle in the face of personal and social change.

531) Rope

Rope is a psychological thriller about two friends who murder a classmate and attempt to get away with the crime by hosting a dinner party with the victim's body in the room.

532) Nosferatu

Nosferatu is a 1922 German Expressionist horror film that follows Count Orlok, a vampire, as he terrorizes a small town in search of his next victim.

533) The Wild Bunch

The Wild Bunch is a classic western about a gang of outlaws on one last mission to take on a corrupt railroad tycoon and his posse.

534) Three Colors: Blue

Three Colors: Blue is a deeply moving story of a woman's journey towards freedom and self-discovery following the death of her husband and daughter.

535) Togo

Togo is a heartwarming adventure film about a legendary sled dog and his musher's quest to save a small Alaskan town from a diphtheria outbreak in 1925.

536) The Manchurian Candidate

The Manchurian Candidate is a 1962 political thriller about a former prisoner of war who is brainwashed into becoming an assassin for a Communist conspiracy.

537) Hero

Hero is a visually stunning martial arts epic about a nameless warrior who must defeat three assassins to save the King of Qin.

538) Dancer in the Dark

Dancer in the Dark is a musical drama about a single mother who is slowly going blind and struggles to protect her son from a similar fate while trying to make enough money to pay for an operation.

539) Patton

Patton tells the story of the controversial World War II General George S. Patton, his successes and failures on and off the battlefield, and his complex relationship with his troops.

540) Notorious

Notorious is a biographical drama about the life of American rapper Christopher Wallace, also known as The Notorious B.I.G.

541) My Left Foot

My Left Foot is a biographical drama about Christy Brown, an Irishman born with cerebral palsy who, with the help of his family and a supportive doctor, learns to write and paint using only his left foot.

542) King Kong

King Kong is a classic monster movie about a giant ape who is brought to New York and falls in love with a beautiful woman.

543) The Conformist

The Conformist is a 1970 Italian drama film about a man who is willing to do whatever it takes to conform to the fascist ideals of 1930s Italy.

544) The Adventures of Robin Hood

The Adventures of Robin Hood is a classic swashbuckling adventure that follows the heroic outlaw Robin Hood as he attempts to outwit the Sheriff of Nottingham and restore justice in England.

545) Once Were Warriors

Once Were Warriors is a powerful and gritty drama about a Maori family struggling to survive in a poverty-stricken urban environment.

546) The Lion in Winter

The Lion in Winter is a historical drama about the Plantagenet royal family as they battle for the throne of England during Christmas 1183.

547) Short Term 12

Short Term 12 is a heartfelt drama about the lives of the staff and residents of a foster care facility, exploring themes of love, trust, and resilience.

548) Strangers on a Train

Strangers on a Train is a psychological thriller about two men who agree to exchange murders, but when one of them reneges on the deal, the other begins to stalk him.

549) Letters from Iwo Jima

Letters from Iwo Jima is a 2006 war drama that follows the story of the Japanese soldiers who fought in the Battle of Iwo Jima during World War II.

550) The Big Sleep

The Big Sleep follows private detective Philip Marlowe as he investigates a complex web of blackmail and murder.

551) The Philadelphia Story

The Philadelphia Story is a romantic comedy about a high society woman who must choose between her ex-husband, a tabloid reporter, and her fiancée on the eve of her wedding.

552) Whisper of the Heart

Whisper of the Heart is a coming-of-age story about a young girl's journey of self-discovery as she follows her dreams and learns to believe in herself.

553) In Cold Blood

In Cold Blood is a crime drama film based on Truman Capote's novel of the same name, following the story of two criminals who commit a quadruple murder in rural Kansas.

554) The Thin Man

The Thin Man is a classic 1930s screwball comedy about a married couple, Nick and Nora Charles, who team up to solve a murder mystery.

555) Amour

Amour is a heartbreaking story of an elderly couple dealing with the physical and emotional effects of aging and illness.

556) Head-On

Head-On is a powerful and tragic story of two troubled souls who find solace in each other, but ultimately struggle to break free from the self-destructive habits that bind them.

557) Talk to Her

Talk to Her is a 2002 Spanish drama film about two men who form a unique friendship while caring for two women in comas.

558) A Taxi Driver

A Taxi Driver is a South Korean drama film about a taxi driver from Seoul who takes a German journalist to the city of Gwangju to cover the 1980 Gwangju Uprising.

559) Arsenic and Old Lace

Arsenic and Old Lace is a dark comedy about two elderly sisters who poison lonely old men with arsenic-laced elderberry wine.

560) 3-Iron

3-Iron is a quiet, contemplative film about a young homeless man and a woman who form an unlikely bond while living on the outskirts of society.

561) Harvey

Harvey is a classic comedy about an eccentric man and his friendship with an invisible 6-foot-tall rabbit.

562) Cat on a Hot Tin Roof

Cat on a Hot Tin Roof is a classic drama about a wealthy Southern family and the secrets they keep from each other.

563) My Name Is Khan

My Name Is Khan is a drama about an autistic Muslim man who embarks on a journey across America to prove his innocence after being falsely accused of terrorism.

564) Laura

Laura is a classic film noir about a detective's investigation into the mysterious death of a beautiful woman.

565) Kal Ho Naa Ho

Kal Ho Naa Ho is a heartwarming romantic comedy-drama about two star-crossed lovers who must overcome family and cultural differences to be together.

566) I Remember

I Remember is a coming-of-age movie about a young girl learning to cope with the death of her mother while navigating the complexities of growing up.

567) The Sacrifice

The Sacrifice is a powerful story of a man's spiritual journey of self-sacrifice for the greater good.

568) Miracle on 34th Street

Miracle on 34th Street is a heartwarming Christmas classic about a department store Santa who may or may not be the real Santa Claus.

569) Nine Queens

Nine Queens is a crime-drama about two con artists who attempt to pull off a major heist in Buenos Aires.

570) In a Lonely Place

In a Lonely Place is a 1950 film noir about a troubled, violent man who is accused of murder and must prove his innocence, while struggling with a potential mental illness.

571) Battleship Potemkin

Battleship Potemkin is a 1925 Soviet silent film about a mutiny by the crew of the Russian battleship Potemkin against their oppressive officers.

572) Gully Boy

Gully Boy is a coming-of-age story of an Indian street rapper from the slums of Mumbai who strives to achieve his dream of becoming a successful rapper.

573) 4 Months, 3 Weeks and 2 Days

4 Months, 3 Weeks and 2 Days is a powerful, emotionally charged drama about a young woman's struggle to help her friend get an illegal abortion in Communist Romania.

574) Kagemusha

Kagemusha is a 1980 Japanese epic historical drama film directed by Akira Kurosawa, about a lower-class criminal who is recruited to impersonate a powerful warlord and unite a divided 16th century Japan.

575) Vivre Sa Vie

Vivre Sa Vie is a French New Wave film about a woman's descent into a life of prostitution and her struggles to find meaning in her life.

576) The Way He Looks

The Way He Looks is a Brazilian coming-of-age drama about a teenage blind boy who falls in love with a new classmate.

577) Mildred Pierce

Mildred Pierce is a 1945 drama film about a single mother struggling to provide for her spoiled daughter during the Great Depression.

578) Le Cercle Rouge

Le Cercle Rouge is a classic French crime drama about a recently released convict, an ex-cop, and a master thief who team up for an ambitious heist.

579) Elevator to the Gallows

Elevator to the Gallows is a French crime drama about a couple who plan a murder, only for their plan to be thrown into chaos when the elevator they use to escape gets stuck.

580) Hiroshima Mon Amour

Hiroshima Mon Amour is a French New Wave drama film that follows a French woman's relationship with a Japanese man in the aftermath of the atomic bombing of Hiroshima.

581) Sullivan's Travels

Sullivan's Travels is a comedy-drama about a Hollywood director who goes on a journey to experience poverty and hardship in order to better understand the struggles of the downtrodden.

582) The Rules of the Game

The Rules of the Game is a French comedy-drama film about a group of wealthy aristocrats whose lives become intertwined over the course of a weekend at a countryside estate.

583) About Elly

About Elly is a suspenseful Iranian drama about a group of friends whose weekend outing takes an unexpected turn when one of them goes missing.

584) The Lost Weekend

The Lost Weekend is a 1945 drama film about an alcoholic writer's four-day struggle with alcoholism and its devastating effects on his life.

585) Jab We Met

Jab We Met is a romantic comedy-drama about two strangers who meet on a train and eventually fall in love.

586) The Big Heat

The Big Heat is a classic film noir about a cop who seeks revenge against a criminal syndicate after his wife is murdered.

587) The Return

The Return is a drama about a young woman who returns home to her family after being away for a decade and must face the consequences of her past.

588) Beauty and the Beast

Beauty and the Beast is a classic Disney animated musical about a young woman who falls in love with a cursed prince who is transformed into a beast.

589) No Man's Land

No Man's Land is a darkly comedic war drama set in the Bosnian War, exploring themes of nationalism, masculinity, and the human cost of war.

590) C.R.A.Z.Y.

C.R.A.Z.Y. is a coming-of-age drama about a gay French-Canadian teenager growing up in 1960s Quebec and struggling to find acceptance from his conservative family.

591) Badhaai Ho

Badhaai Ho is a heartwarming comedy-drama about a middle-aged couple who must come to terms with an unexpected pregnancy and the reactions of their family and society.

592) Dev.D

Dev.D is a modern adaptation of the classic novel Devdas that follows the story of a young man's journey of self-discovery and redemption.

593) M.S. Dhoni: The Untold Story

M.S. Dhoni: The Untold Story is a biopic that follows the journey of Indian cricketer Mahendra Singh Dhoni from his humble beginnings to becoming one of the most successful captains of the Indian cricket team.

594) Super 30

Super 30 is a biographical drama about the life of Indian mathematician Anand Kumar and his educational program of the same name, which helps underprivileged students prepare for the IIT entrance exam.

595) Airlift

Airlift is a thrilling and inspiring story of one man's extraordinary mission to evacuate over 170,000 Indians from Kuwait during the 1990 Iraqi invasion.

596) Pad Man

Pad Man is a heartwarming and inspiring story about a man's quest to revolutionize menstrual hygiene in India.

597) Baby

Baby is a coming-of-age story about an 18-year-old girl who must choose between her dreams of becoming a dancer and the pressure of her family to conform to their traditional values.

598) Avatar: The Way of Water

Avatar: The Way of Water is a sci-fi action adventure film about a young woman who embarks on a quest to save her people from an oppressive corporate force by harnessing the power of nature.

599) The Banshees of Inisherin

The Banshees of Inisherin is a dark fantasy adventure about a young girl's journey to save her village from a curse.

600) Aftersun

Aftersun is a romantic drama about a young couple who struggle to find their place in the world after their relationship is tested by a life-altering event.

601) All Quiet on the Western Front

All Quiet on the Western Front is a powerful anti-war drama that follows a group of German soldiers during World War I as they struggle to survive in the trenches.

602) The Batman

The Batman is a superhero action film about Bruce Wayne's transformation into the Dark Knight and his fight against Gotham City's most notorious villains.

603) The Gentlemen

The Gentlemen follows a British drug lord who is trying to sell his empire to a dynasty of billionaires, and finds himself in a web of deceit and danger in the process.

604) Drive

Drive is a neo-noir crime thriller about a Hollywood stunt driver who moonlights as a getaway driver for criminals.

605) Tombstone

The movie Tombstone is a Western drama about the legendary lawman Wyatt Earp and his struggle to maintain law and order in the Wild West town of Tombstone, Arizona.

606) The Breakfast Club

The Breakfast Club is a classic coming of age story about five high school students from different backgrounds who come together for a Saturday detention and learn to accept and understand one another.

607) Pride & Prejudice

Pride & Prejudice is a classic romantic comedy about Elizabeth Bennet, who must navigate her feelings for the proud Mr. Darcy, while dealing with the expectations of marriage in 19th century English society.

608) Hidden Figures

Hidden Figures is a biographical drama about the African-American women who played a crucial role in NASA's successful launch of astronaut John Glenn into orbit in 1962.

609) Rogue One: A Star Wars Story

Rogue One: A Star Wars Story is a spin-off prequel that follows a group of rebels on a mission to steal the plans to the Death Star.

610) Little Women

Little Women is a classic coming-of-age story about four sisters growing up in Civil War-era America and learning to navigate life's challenges and joys.

611) The Worst Person in the World

The Worst Person in the World is a dark comedy about a man who is forced to confront his own selfishness and narcissism when he is confronted by a stranger who claims to be the worst person in the world.

612) Thirteen Lives

Thirteen Lives is a documentary about the 2018 Tham Luang cave rescue mission in Thailand, which saved 12 boys and their soccer coach from a flooded cave system.

613) About Time

About Time is a romantic comedy-drama about a man who discovers he can travel back in time and use the knowledge to shape his future.

614) The Hateful Eight

The Hateful Eight is a western mystery film about a group of strangers who become stranded in a haberdashery during a blizzard, and must confront their dark pasts in order to survive.

615) The Hobbit: An Unexpected Journey

The Hobbit: An Unexpected Journey is an adventure film following Bilbo Baggins on a quest to reclaim the lost Dwarf Kingdom of Erebor from the dragon Smaug.

616) Call Me by Your Name

Call Me by Your Name is a coming-of-age romantic drama about a young man's summer of self-discovery and love in Northern Italy.

617) The Big Short

The Big Short is a comedic drama about four outsiders who bet against the housing market and make a fortune when it collapses during the financial crisis of 2007-2008.

618) The Irishman

The Irishman is a crime drama about an aging mob hitman who reflects on his past life and regrets the choices he made.

619) Dunkirk

Dunkirk is a thrilling WWII drama that follows the evacuation of Allied soldiers from the beaches of Dunkirk, France, as they are surrounded by the enemy.

620) Star Wars: Episode VII - The Force Awakens

The Force Awakens follows the journey of Rey, Finn, and Poe as they join forces with the

Resistance to defeat the First Order and restore balance to the Force.

621) The Notebook

The Notebook is a romantic drama about two star-crossed lovers who stay together despite all odds.

622) Ghostbusters

Ghostbusters is a classic comedy about a group of scientists who start a ghost-catching business in New York City.

623) Remember the Titans

Remember the Titans is a sports drama that follows the story of a newly-integrated high school football team and their struggles to overcome prejudice and form a unified team.

624) Nightcrawler

Nightcrawler is a crime thriller that follows a desperate young man who finds work as a freelance crime journalist in the nocturnal underbelly of Los Angeles.

625) The Social Network

The Social Network is a movie about the creation of Facebook and the personal and legal struggles of its founder, Mark Zuckerberg.

626) The Girl with the Dragon Tattoo

The Girl with the Dragon Tattoo follows a journalist and a young computer hacker as they investigate the disappearance of a wealthy patriarch's niece, uncovering dark family secrets along the way.

627) Little Miss Sunshine

Little Miss Sunshine is a heartwarming comedy-drama about a dysfunctional family on a road trip to get their daughter to a beauty pageant.

628) Apocalypto

Apocalypto is a thrilling adventure story set in 16th century Mesoamerica, that follows a young man as he embarks on a daring quest to save his people from an oppressive empire.

629) Skyfall

Skyfall follows James Bond as he battles a mysterious villain who is determined to destroy MI6 and the legacy of Bond's mentor, M.

630) Ferris Bueller's Day Off

Ferris Bueller's Day Off is a comedy about a high school student who skips school for a day of fun and adventure with his friends in Chicago.

631) Atonement

Atonement is a romantic drama about a young girl's false accusation that tears apart the lives of two lovers.

632) Manchester by the Sea

Manchester by the Sea is a poignant drama about a man who is forced to confront his past after returning to his hometown to take care of his teenage nephew.

633) The Hobbit: The Desolation of Smaug

The Hobbit: The Desolation of Smaug follows Bilbo Baggins and a group of dwarves on their quest to reclaim their homeland from the dragon Smaug.

634) Predator

An elite team of soldiers is hunted by a mysterious, technologically advanced alien hunter in the jungles of Central America.

635) The Curious Case of Benjamin Button

The Curious Case of Benjamin Button is a fantasy drama about a man who is born an elderly man and ages in reverse.

636) The Fugitive

The Fugitive is a thrilling action-adventure film about a doctor falsely accused of murdering his wife, who must evade the law to prove his innocence.

637) Crash

Crash is a drama about the complex relationships between people of different races, classes, and genders in Los Angeles, and how they intersect in unexpected ways.

638) The Last Samurai

The Last Samurai is a historical drama set in 19th century Japan, following the story of an American military advisor who is drawn into the way of the samurai.

639) The Untouchables

The Untouchables is a crime drama about a team of federal agents in prohibition-era Chicago who take on the city's most notorious gangster, Al Capone.

640) Cast Away

Cast Away is a drama about a FedEx executive who is stranded on a deserted island after his plane crashes in the South Pacific.

641) Mr. Nobody

Mr. Nobody is a sci-fi drama about a 118-year-old man reflecting on his life and the choices he has made.

642) Taken

Taken is an action-packed thriller about a retired CIA agent who must use his particular set of skills to save his daughter from human traffickers.

643) The Sandlot

The Sandlot is a coming-of-age movie about a group of young baseball players and their summer adventures in 1962.

644) Captain America: Civil War

Captain America: Civil War is a Marvel movie that follows the Avengers as they are divided into two opposing factions over a political disagreement, leading to a dramatic showdown between them.

645) Hot Fuzz

Hot Fuzz is an action-comedy about a top London cop who is reassigned to a small town and discovers a sinister conspiracy is afoot.

646) Willy Wonka & the Chocolate Factory

Willy Wonka & the Chocolate Factory is a classic musical fantasy film about a young boy who wins a tour of a mysterious chocolate factory run by a eccentric chocolatier.

647) The Fighter

The Fighter is a biographical drama about the rise of boxer ""Irish"" Micky Ward and his struggle to overcome personal and professional obstacles on his way to a world championship title.

648) Back to the Future Part II

The sequel to Back to the Future follows Marty McFly and Doc Brown as they travel to the future to save Marty's future family from disaster.

649) Captain America: The Winter Soldier

Captain America: The Winter Soldier is an action-packed superhero movie that follows Steve Rogers as he battles a mysterious assassin known as the Winter Soldier while also uncovering a dangerous conspiracy.

650) Mary Poppins

Mary Poppins is a classic musical fantasy film about a magical nanny who uses her unique magical powers to help a family rediscover the joy in life.

651) Isle of Dogs

Isle of Dogs is an animated stop-motion adventure comedy about a boy's quest to find his lost dog on a trash-filled island of exiled canines.

652) Serenity

Serenity is a sci-fi action-adventure film about a band of renegade space travelers who must fight to survive in a dangerous universe.

653) Captain Fantastic

Captain Fantastic is a heartwarming comedy-drama about a family living off the grid in the Pacific Northwest and their struggles to balance their unconventional lifestyle with the demands of society.

654) I Saw the Devil

I Saw the Devil is a violent revenge thriller about a secret agent who hunts down the serial killer who murdered his fiancée.

655) Misery

Misery is a psychological thriller about a famous novelist who is held captive by a deranged fan who forces him to write a book to her liking.

656) A Bronx Tale

A Bronx Tale is a coming-of-age drama about a young Italian-American boy who struggles to choose between the temptations of organized crime and the values of his hard-working father.

657) American Gangster

American Gangster is a crime drama about a drug kingpin in 1970s Harlem who rises to power and must face the consequences of his criminal lifestyle.

658) The Holy Mountain

The Holy Mountain is a surrealist film that follows a group of people on a spiritual journey to find enlightenment.

659) Gattaca

Gattaca is a sci-fi drama that follows a genetically inferior man who strives to defy a flawed genetic destiny by assuming the identity of a superior one.

660) Big Hero 6

Big Hero 6 is an animated action-adventure comedy about a group of brilliant young inventors who team up with a lovable robot to save their city from a dangerous villain.

661) Paddington 2

Paddington 2 is a heartwarming family comedy about the beloved bear's misadventures as he searches for the perfect gift for his Aunt Lucy's 100th birthday.

662) Walk the Line

Walk the Line is a biographical drama about legendary country singer Johnny Cash, chronicling his rise to fame and his tumultuous personal life.

663) Moon

Moon is a sci-fi drama about an astronaut who discovers a secret that could change the course of humanity.

664) Moonrise Kingdom

Moonrise Kingdom is a quirky coming-of-age story about two young lovers who run away together in search of a place to call their own.

665) Captain Phillips

Captain Phillips is a thrilling drama about a cargo ship captain who is taken hostage by Somali pirates and must use his wits to survive.

666) Boyz n the Hood

Boyz n the Hood is a powerful coming-of-age drama about three friends growing up in a tough South Central Los Angeles neighborhood.

667) Straight Outta Compton

Straight Outta Compton is a biographical drama about the rise and fall of the influential rap group N.W.A. in the late 1980s and early 1990s.

668) Being John Malkovich

Being John Malkovich is a surreal dark comedy about a puppeteer who discovers a portal that leads into the mind of actor John Malkovich.

669) Midnight Cowboy

Midnight Cowboy is a film about a naive hustler from Texas who moves to New York City in search of wealth and success, but instead finds himself in a world of loneliness and despair.

670) The Killing Fields

The Killing Fields is a powerful drama about the horrors of the Khmer Rouge's reign in Cambodia and the friendship between two journalists, one Cambodian and one American.

671) The Conversation

The Conversation is a psychological thriller about a surveillance expert who is hired to secretly record a conversation, only to find himself drawn into a moral dilemma.

672) The Day of the Jackal

The Day of the Jackal is a 1973 political thriller film about an assassin hired to kill French President Charles de Gaulle.

673) Awakenings

Awakenings is a drama about a doctor who uses a new drug to help catatonic patients come out of their comas and experience life again.

674) Hunt for the Wilderpeople

Hunt for the Wilderpeople is a heartwarming and humorous adventure of a defiant boy and his foster uncle who go on the run in the New Zealand bush.

675) The Girl with the Dragon Tattoo

The Girl with the Dragon Tattoo is a psychological thriller about a journalist and a computer hacker who team up to solve a decades-old murder mystery.

676) How to Train Your Dragon 2

The sequel to How to Train Your Dragon follows Hiccup and Toothless as they journey to discover a secret ice cave that is home to hundreds of new wild dragons and the mysterious Dragon Rider.

677) Glory

Glory is a powerful and inspiring drama about the 54th Massachusetts Volunteer Infantry, the first all-black regiment in the United States Civil War.

678) The Fall

The Fall is a visually stunning, imaginative journey that follows a little girl's journey to help a wounded stuntman heal his broken spirit.

679) The King of Comedy

The King of Comedy is a dark comedy about a delusional aspiring comedian who attempts to kidnap a famous talk show host in order to gain fame and recognition.

680) Kiki's Delivery Service

Kiki's Delivery Service is an animated coming-of-age story about a young witch who moves to a new city and starts a delivery service to help her find her place in the world.

681) The Best Offer

The Best Offer is a psychological drama about a reclusive art auctioneer who is drawn into a mysterious and dangerous world when he takes on the case of a mysterious woman.

682) Dawn of the Dead

Dawn of the Dead is a horror movie about a group of survivors struggling to stay alive while being surrounded by hordes of zombies.

683) The Outlaw Josey Wales

The Outlaw Josey Wales is a western revenge story in which a Missouri farmer joins a Confederate guerrilla unit and winds up on the run from the Union soldiers who murdered his family.

684) The Remains of the Day

The Remains of the Day is a 1993 drama about an English butler's struggle to reconcile his professional duty with his personal desires.

685) My Fair Lady

My Fair Lady is a musical romantic comedy-drama based on the play by George Bernard Shaw, about a Cockney flower girl who is transformed into an elegant lady with the help of a linguistics professor.

686) Cabaret

Cabaret is a musical drama set in 1930s Berlin that follows the story of a young English cabaret singer and her relationships with a wealthy playboy and a Jewish fruit vendor.

687) Mississippi Burning

Mississippi Burning is a powerful drama about two FBI agents who investigate the disappearance of three civil rights activists in a small town in Mississippi in 1964.

688) The Insider

The Insider is a 1999 drama film about a tobacco industry whistleblower who risks his life to expose the truth about the company's practices.

689) Night of the Living Dead

Night of the Living Dead is a horror classic about a group of people trapped in a farmhouse who must fight off an onslaught of flesh-eating zombies.

690) The Day the Earth Stood Still

The Day the Earth Stood Still is a sci-fi classic about an alien who visits Earth to deliver a warning to the human race to stop their destructive behavior or face dire consequences.

691) Once

Once is a romantic musical drama about an Irish street musician and a Czech immigrant who form an unexpected bond while trying to make their dreams come true.

692) Changeling

Changeling is a 2008 crime drama film based on the true story of a mother's fight to prove the LAPD's mistake in returning the wrong boy after her son's disappearance.

693) Kramer vs. Kramer

Kramer vs. Kramer is a drama about a divorcing couple who must learn to put aside their differences for the sake of their son.

694) The Right Stuff

The Right Stuff is a biographical drama about the first American astronauts and their journey to becoming the first people in space.

695) All That Jazz

All That Jazz is a semi-autobiographical musical drama about a talented yet self-destructive choreographer and director struggling with his personal and professional life.

696) Hamlet

Hamlet is a tragedy about a young prince who must avenge his father's death and deal with the consequences of his actions.

697) Ed Wood

Ed Wood is a biographical comedy-drama about the life and career of the infamous B-movie director, Edward D. Wood Jr.

698) Breaking the Waves

Breaking the Waves is a powerful drama about a woman's faith and love being tested when her husband is seriously injured in an accident.

699) Stagecoach

Stagecoach follows a group of strangers who must band together to survive dangerous circumstances while travelling through dangerous Apache territory.

700) Pride

Pride is a heartwarming comedy-drama about a group of LGBT activists in Britain who come together to support a small Welsh mining village in their struggle against Margaret Thatcher's government in the 1980s.

701) Days of Heaven

Days of Heaven is a romantic drama set in early 20th century Texas, about a young couple who flee to the Texas Panhandle to escape poverty and find themselves caught in a love triangle with a wealthy farmer.

702) Gaslight

Gaslight is a psychological thriller about a woman whose husband manipulates her into believing she is going insane in order to get her out of the way and steal her inheritance.

703) Mother

Mother is a psychological thriller about a couple whose relationship is tested when an unnerving outsider comes to stay with them.

704) October Sky

October Sky is a coming-of-age drama about a group of boys in a small mining town in West Virginia who are inspired by the launch of Sputnik to pursue their dreams of becoming rocket scientists.

705) Freaks

Freaks is a 1932 horror film about a group of carnival sideshow performers who band together to protect one of their own from an evil trapeze artist.

706) Frankenstein

Frankenstein is a horror story about a scientist who creates a monster from dead body parts and the consequences of his actions.

707) The Man Who Would Be King

The Man Who Would Be King is a classic adventure tale about two British soldiers who set out to become kings in the wilds of 19th-century India.

708) The Chaser

The Chaser follows a former detective's desperate attempt to rescue a kidnapped girl from a dangerous criminal.

709) Lilya 4-Ever

Lilya 4-Ever is a heartbreaking story about a young girl who is forced to grow up too quickly and must fight for her survival in an unforgiving world.

710) Guess Who's Coming to Dinner

Guess Who's Coming to Dinner is a 1967 romantic comedy-drama about an interracial couple whose parents must come to terms with their relationship.

711) East of Eden

East of Eden is a classic drama about two brothers competing for the love and approval of their father in the Salinas Valley of California.

712) Loving Vincent

Loving Vincent is a biographical animated drama film about the life and death of Vincent van Gogh, told through the use of oil paintings in the style of his artwork.

713) Hannah and Her Sisters

Hannah and Her Sisters is a story about the complexities of relationships between three sisters, their husbands, and their parents as they all navigate life together.

714) Bringing Up Baby

Bringing Up Baby is a classic screwball comedy about a paleontologist, a socialite, and a leopard that hilariously disrupts their lives.

715) Batman: Mask of the Phantasm

Batman: Mask of the Phantasm is an animated movie about Bruce Wayne's struggle to balance his dual identities as Batman and Bruce Wayne while trying to clear his name from a series of murders.

716) Red River

Red River is an epic Western about a cattle drive led by a stubborn and proud rancher and his adopted son that leads to a clash of wills and a journey of self-discovery.

717) Manhattan

Manhattan is a romantic comedy-drama about a neurotic writer's complicated relationship with a 17-year-old girl and his own mid-life crisis.

718) His Girl Friday

His Girl Friday is a classic screwball comedy about an ex-husband and wife team of reporters who must outwit each other to get the scoop on a major story.

719) The Bride of Frankenstein

The Bride of Frankenstein is a classic horror film about a mad scientist and his creation of a female monster in an attempt to create the perfect mate for his original creation.

720) Aguirre, the Wrath of God

Aguirre, the Wrath of God is a 1972 German epic historical drama film about a deranged Spanish conquistador who leads a group of conquistadors on a disastrous mission down the Amazon River in search of the legendary City of Gold.

721) All About My Mother

All About My Mother is a Spanish drama that follows a mother's journey to reconnect with her estranged son after he is killed in a car accident.

722) The White Ribbon

The White Ribbon is a dark drama set in a German village before World War I, exploring themes of innocence, morality, and the consequences of oppressive religious control.

723) The World's Fastest Indian

The World's Fastest Indian is a heartwarming story about an elderly man's journey to fulfill his dream of racing his beloved motorcycle at the Bonneville Salt Flats in Utah.

724) I, Daniel Blake

I, Daniel Blake is a heartbreaking story about an elderly man's struggle to receive benefits from a bureaucratic system that fails to recognize his needs.

725) The Discreet Charm of the Bourgeoisie

The Discreet Charm of the Bourgeoisie is a surrealist comedy about a group of upper-class friends whose attempts to have dinner together are continually thwarted by bizarre occurrences.

726) Shadow of a Doubt

Shadow of a Doubt is a psychological thriller about a young girl who discovers that her beloved uncle may not be the man she thought he was.

727) Land of Mine

Land of Mine is a powerful and emotional drama about a group of young German POWs who are forced to disarm land mines in post-WWII Denmark.

728) The Lady Vanishes

The Lady Vanishes is a 1938 British thriller about a young woman's search for an elderly woman who mysteriously disappears on a train ride.

729) A Prophet

A Prophet is a powerful drama about a young man's journey from naive rookie to hardened criminal in a French prison.

730) To Have and Have Not

To Have and Have Not is a classic romantic drama set in Martinique during World War II, following the story of a fisherman and a young woman who fall in love despite the dangers of the war.

731) The Umbrellas of Cherbourg

The Umbrellas of Cherbourg is a musical romance about two young lovers who are tragically separated by life's circumstances.

732) Cowboy Bebop: The Movie

Cowboy Bebop: The Movie is an action-packed sci-fi adventure about a group of bounty hunters chasing a dangerous terrorist through space.

733) The Lunchbox

The Lunchbox is a heartwarming story of two strangers who form an unexpected bond through a mistaken delivery of a lunchbox.

734) L'avventura

L'avventura follows a group of friends on a search for a missing woman on a remote Mediterranean island, leading to a mysterious and ambiguous conclusion.

735) The Chorus

The Chorus is a French drama about a music teacher who helps a group of troubled boys find hope and redemption through the power of song.

736) Ninja Scroll

Ninja Scroll is an action-packed anime movie about a ninja's quest to save Japan from demonic forces.

737) Like Father, Like Son

Like Father, Like Son is a heartwarming story about two fathers who must come to terms with the fact that their sons were switched at birth.

738) The Asphalt Jungle

The Asphalt Jungle is a classic crime drama following a group of criminals as they plan and execute a daring heist, with unexpected consequences.

739) You Can't Take It with You

You Can't Take It with You is a comedy about a chaotic family living in an old house who are thrown into chaos when the daughter falls in love with a man from a conservative, wealthy family.

740) Tokyo Godfathers

Tokyo Godfathers is an anime film about three homeless people who discover an abandoned baby and set out on a heartwarming journey to find its parents.

741) The Killer

The Killer is an action-packed thriller about an assassin who must confront his past in order to protect an innocent woman from a powerful crime lord.

742) The Innocents

The Innocents is a psychological horror film about a governess who discovers that the two children she is caring for are being possessed by ghosts.

743) Millennium Actress

Millennium Actress is a surrealistic, animated love story about an aging actress, Chiyoko, and her lifelong quest to find a mysterious man from her past.

744) Crimes and Misdemeanors

Crimes and Misdemeanors is an exploration of morality, justice, and the consequences of our choices in life.

745) Once Upon a Time in Anatolia

Once Upon a Time in Anatolia is a slow-paced, contemplative drama about a group of men searching for a body in the Anatolian steppes.

746) The Postman

The Postman is a post-apocalyptic drama about a drifter who brings hope to a small community by impersonating a postman from the restored United States government.

747) Duck Soup

Duck Soup is a madcap Marx Brothers comedy that follows the chaotic antics of a small country's leader and his bumbling cabinet as they try to outwit their enemy.

748) Knockin' on Heaven's Door

Knockin' on Heaven's Door is a German crime drama about two young men who become involved in a bank robbery and must face the consequences of their actions.

749) Veer-Zaara

Veer-Zaara is a romantic drama about the love story of an Indian Air Force pilot and a Pakistani woman who are separated by circumstances beyond their control.

750) Hindi Medium

Hindi Medium is a heartwarming comedy-drama about a couple's struggle to provide their daughter with a good education in a society obsessed with English.

751) A Night at the Opera

A Night at the Opera is a classic Marx Brothers comedy about a group of performers trying to save an opera company from financial ruin.

752) Vicky Donor

Vicky Donor is a light-hearted romantic comedy about a sperm donor who finds love and acceptance in a traditional Indian family.

753) English Vinglish

English Vinglish is a heartwarming comedy-drama about a middle-aged Indian woman's journey of self-discovery and empowerment as she learns to speak English.

754) The Fabelmans

The Fabelmans is a heartwarming story about a family of musicians struggling to keep their traditions alive in the face of modern society.

755) Guillermo del Toro's Pinocchio

Guillermo del Toro's Pinocchio is a dark fantasy re-imagining of the classic story of a wooden puppet's quest to become a real boy.

756) The Goonies

The Goonies is a classic family adventure film about a group of misfit kids who embark on a treasure hunt to save their homes from foreclosure.

757) A Man Called Ove

A Man Called Ove is a heartwarming comedy-drama about a grumpy old man who finds joy and purpose in life through the relationships he forms with his neighbors.

758) Road to Perdition

Road to Perdition is a film about a father and son's journey of redemption and revenge in 1930s America.

759) Get Out

Get Out is a horror-thriller that follows a young African-American man as he discovers a disturbing secret about the family of his white girlfriend.

760) Harry Potter and the Goblet of Fire

Harry Potter must compete in a dangerous tournament between three wizarding schools and face a deadly dragon, all while dealing with the rising threat of Lord Voldemort.

761) Mission: Impossible - Fallout

Mission: Impossible - Fallout is an action-packed spy thriller following Ethan Hunt and his team as they race against time to stop a dangerous terrorist organization from acquiring nuclear weapons.

762) Wind River

Wind River is a crime drama set in the Wyoming wilderness, in which a rookie FBI agent teams up with a game tracker to investigate a murder on a Native American reservation.

763) Harry Potter and the Deathly Hallows: Part 1

Harry Potter and the Deathly Hallows: Part 1 follows Harry, Ron, and Hermione as they search for the Horcruxes in an effort to defeat Lord Voldemort and save the wizarding world.

764) Ex Machina

Ex Machina is a science fiction drama about a programmer who is invited to test the human-like capabilities of a highly advanced artificial intelligence.

765) Kingsman: The Secret Service

Kingsman: The Secret Service is a spy action-comedy film about a secret agent organization that recruits an unrefined street kid into their ranks.

766) Brokeback Mountain

Brokeback Mountain tells the story of two cowboys who fall in love and struggle to keep their relationship a secret in a society that is not accepting of their love.

767) Zodiac

Zodiac is a crime drama that follows the story of a serial killer in San Francisco in the late 1960s and early 1970s, as the police attempt to identify and capture the killer.

768) The Hangover

The Hangover is a comedy about four friends who go on a wild bachelor party in Las Vegas and must piece together the events of the night before to find their missing friend.

769) Primal Fear

Primal Fear is a courtroom drama about an altar boy accused of murdering an influential lawyer, and the defense attorney's struggle to uncover the truth.

770) Home Alone

An eight-year-old boy is accidentally left home alone and must defend his house from two bumbling burglars.

771) Ocean's Eleven

An all-star cast of criminals come together to pull off an elaborate heist of three Las Vegas casinos owned by their nemesis.

772) Airplane!

Airplane! is a classic comedy film about a former fighter pilot who must save a plane full of passengers from a variety of disasters.

773) Black Hawk Down

Black Hawk Down is a war drama depicting the 1993 US military raid in Mogadishu, Somalia, and the ensuing battle between US forces and Somali militia.

774) Blue Is the Warmest Colour

Blue Is the Warmest Colour is a coming-of-age drama about a teenage girl who discovers her own sexuality and identity through a passionate relationship with an older woman.

775) Deadpool 2

Deadpool 2 is an action-packed, irreverent superhero comedy that follows the foul-mouthed mercenary as he teams up with a group of mutants to protect a young boy from a time-traveling cyborg.

776) What's Eating Gilbert Grape

What's Eating Gilbert Grape is a coming-of-age drama about a young man struggling to take care of his family while trying to find his own identity.

777) The Game

The Game is a psychological thriller about a wealthy investment banker who is given a mysterious and manipulative game as a birthday present.

778) Blue Velvet

Blue Velvet is a neo-noir mystery film that follows a college student as he discovers the dark secrets of a small town after finding a severed human ear in a field.

779) Another Round

Another Round is a Danish comedy-drama about four friends who embark on an experiment to see if alcohol can improve their lives.

780) 500 Days of Summer

500 Days of Summer is a romantic comedy-drama that follows the relationship between a young man and woman as they navigate the ups and downs of their relationship over the course of 500 days.

781) Birdman or (The Unexpected Virtue of Ignorance)

Birdman is a darkly comedic drama about an actor struggling to reclaim his past fame while contending with his inner demons.

782) When Harry Met Sally...

When Harry Met Sally is a romantic comedy about two friends who struggle to maintain their friendship despite developing romantic feelings for one another.

783) O Brother, Where Art Thou?

O Brother, Where Art Thou is a comedic adventure of three escaped convicts on a quest for buried treasure in Depression-era Mississippi.

784) A Few Good Men

A Few Good Men is a courtroom drama about a military trial that examines the moral responsibility of following orders.

785) Lost in Translation

Lost in Translation is a poignant and humorous exploration of two strangers' unlikely friendship as they find solace in a foreign city.

786) Blazing Saddles

Blazing Saddles is a classic Western comedy about a black sheriff who must save a small town from a corrupt politician.

787) Sound of Metal

Sound of Metal follows a heavy metal drummer's journey to come to terms with his sudden hearing loss and find a new life path.

788) Tangled

Tangled is an animated Disney movie about a princess who embarks on a journey to find her true identity with the help of a thief.

789) Gravity

Gravity is a thrilling and suspenseful drama about two astronauts struggling to survive in space after their space shuttle is destroyed.

790) Empire of the Sun

Empire of the Sun is a coming-of-age story set in World War II Shanghai, following a young boy's journey of survival and self-discovery.

791) Deliverance

Deliverance is a 1972 American thriller film about four city dwellers who embark on a weekend canoe trip in the Georgia wilderness and are confronted with danger, unexpected danger, and the ultimate test of their survival skills.

792) Clerks

Clerks is a black comedy about two convenience store clerks and their often absurd conversations and interactions with customers.

793) The Machinist

The Machinist is a psychological thriller about an insomniac machinist whose physical and mental health deteriorate as he becomes increasingly paranoid and obsessed with the idea that he is being stalked by a mysterious figure.

794) Training Day

Training Day is a crime thriller about a rookie cop who is forced to confront the dark side of law enforcement when he is assigned to shadow a morally ambiguous veteran detective.

795) Y tu mamá también

Y tu mamá también is a Mexican coming-of-age drama that follows two teenage boys on a road trip of self-discovery with an older woman.

796) Halloween

Halloween is a horror film about a serial killer who escapes from a mental institution and returns to his hometown to murder unsuspecting teenagers.

797) The Last of the Mohicans

The Last of the Mohicans is an action-packed historical drama about a group of British colonists in the American wilderness during the French and Indian War, and their struggle for survival against the odds.

798) Coraline

Coraline is a dark fantasy adventure film about a young girl who discovers a secret, fantastical world behind a secret door in her new home.

799) Donnie Brasco

Donnie Brasco is a crime drama about an undercover FBI agent who infiltrates the mafia and forms a deep bond with the mobster he is assigned to investigate.

800) Silver Linings Playbook

Silver Linings Playbook is a romantic comedy-drama about a man with bipolar disorder who attempts to rebuild his life and find love after being released from a mental institution.

801) The Magnificent Seven

The Magnificent Seven is a classic western about seven gunslingers who come together to protect a small town from a ruthless robber baron.

802) X-Men: First Class

X-Men: First Class follows the story of how Professor Xavier and Magneto's relationship is tested when they must choose between their duty to save humanity and their fight for mutant rights.

803) First Blood

John Rambo, a former Green Beret, uses his special skills to survive in a small town while being pursued by a relentless sheriff.

804) The Boy in the Striped Pajamas

The Boy in the Striped Pajamas is a powerful and heartbreaking story about the friendship between two young boys, one Jewish and one German, during the Holocaust.

805) The Count of Monte Cristo

The Count of Monte Cristo is a classic tale of revenge, justice, and redemption, as a wrongfully imprisoned man escapes and seeks revenge on those who betrayed him.

806) The Lego Movie

The Lego Movie is an animated adventure comedy about an ordinary Lego minifigure who is thrust into a world of excitement when he is identified as the most extraordinary person and the key to saving the Lego universe.

807) Midnight in Paris

Midnight in Paris is a romantic fantasy comedy-drama about a screenwriter who travels back in time to 1920s Paris and meets some of the era's most famous writers and artists.

808) Sense and Sensibility

Sense and Sensibility is a romantic drama that follows two sisters as they navigate through societal expectations and changing fortunes to find true love.

809) Argo

Argo is a thrilling drama based on the true story of a daring CIA mission to rescue six American diplomats from Iran during the 1979 hostage crisis.

810) Lucky Number Slevin

Lucky Number Slevin is a neo-noir crime thriller about a case of mistaken identity that leads to a dangerous game of cat and mouse between two rival crime lords.

811) 3:10 to Yuma

3:10 to Yuma is a Western drama about a struggling rancher who takes on the task of escorting a dangerous outlaw to justice.

812) Toy Story 4

Toy Story 4 follows Woody, Buzz, and the rest of the toy gang on a heartwarming journey as they confront the struggles of growing up and learning to let go.

813) The Fault in Our Stars

The Fault in Our Stars is a romantic drama about two teenagers with cancer who fall in love and learn to live life to the fullest despite their circumstances.

814) As Good as It Gets

As Good as It Gets is a romantic comedy-drama about a misanthropic, obsessive-compulsive novelist who forms an unlikely bond with a single mother and his gay neighbor.

815) Apollo 13

Apollo 13 is a gripping drama based on the true story of the ill-fated 1970 lunar mission, in which a team of astronauts and engineers work together to overcome seemingly insurmountable odds and return safely to Earth.

816) Wreck-It Ralph

Wreck-It Ralph is an animated adventure comedy about a video game villain who embarks on a quest to become a hero.

817) Who Framed Roger Rabbit

Who Framed Roger Rabbit is a film about a cartoon rabbit who has been framed for murder and must prove his innocence with the help of a human detective.

818) Star Trek II: The Wrath of Khan

Star Trek II: The Wrath of Khan is an action-packed sci-fi adventure that follows the Enterprise crew as they battle the vengeful Khan and his followers.

819) Man on Fire

Man on Fire is a revenge story about a former assassin-turned-bodyguard who takes it upon himself to avenge the kidnapping of the young girl he was hired to protect.

820) The Boondock Saints

The Boondock Saints is a crime action-thriller about two Irish brothers who take justice into their own hands and become vigilantes.

821) Evil Dead II

Evil Dead II is a horror-comedy sequel to the 1981 cult classic, in which a man must battle against a horde of evil deadites to save himself and his girlfriend.

822) Glengarry Glen Ross

Glengarry Glen Ross is a drama about a group of desperate real estate salesmen who will go to any lengths to succeed in their cutthroat business.

823) The Bourne Supremacy

The Bourne Supremacy follows Jason Bourne as he is framed for a CIA operation gone wrong and must outrun and outwit his pursuers in order to clear his name.

824) The Theory of Everything

The Theory of Everything is a biographical drama about the life of renowned physicist Stephen Hawking and his relationship with his first wife, Jane Hawking.

825) Flipped

Flipped is a coming-of-age story about two eighth graders who develop a friendship and eventually fall in love.

826) Star Trek Into Darkness

Star Trek Into Darkness follows the crew of the Enterprise as they battle an unstoppable force of terror from within their own organization.

827) The Verdict

The Verdict is a courtroom drama about an alcoholic lawyer who takes on a medical malpractice case and must fight for justice for his client.

828) Fried Green Tomatoes

Fried Green Tomatoes is a heartwarming story of friendship, courage, and the power of family, set in the American South during the 1920s and 1980s.

829) The Trial of the Chicago 7

The Trial of the Chicago 7 is a historical drama that follows the trial of seven defendants charged with conspiracy and inciting a riot at the 1968 Democratic National Convention in

Chicago.

830) Adaptation.

Adaptation is a dark comedy-drama about a struggling screenwriter who attempts to adapt a book into a screenplay while struggling with his own insecurities and creative frustrations.

831) Roma

Roma is a deeply moving and visually stunning film about a young indigenous woman's journey of self-discovery in 1970s Mexico City.

832) Happiness

Happiness is a dark comedy-drama that follows the lives of three sisters and their dysfunctional family as they grapple with their own personal issues and struggles.

833) Serpico

Serpico is a 1973 crime drama film based on the true story of an honest New York City police officer who risks his life to expose the corruption of his fellow officers.

834) Billy Elliot

Billy Elliot is a heart-warming story about an 11-year-old boy who discovers his passion for ballet despite his family's disapproval.

835) Philadelphia

Philadelphia is a 1993 drama film about a gay lawyer who is fired from his firm because of his HIV-positive status and his fight to regain his job and dignity.

836) The French Connection

The French Connection follows NYPD detectives Popeye Doyle and Cloudy Russo as they attempt to take down a French drug smuggling ring.

837) The Longest Day

The Longest Day is a 1962 epic war film about the D-Day invasion of Normandy during World War II.

838) Naked

Naked is a dark comedy about a man who wakes up the morning after his wedding day, naked in an elevator, and has to piece together the events of the night before in order to discover what happened.

839) The Dirty Dozen

The Dirty Dozen is a classic war film about a group of convicted criminals who are recruited to carry out a dangerous mission during World War II.

840) Goldfinger

The 1964 James Bond film ""Goldfinger"" follows 007 as he investigates the villainous Auric Goldfinger, who is plotting to contaminate the U.S. gold reserves.

841) Dirty Harry

Dirty Harry is a gritty crime drama that follows a renegade cop as he takes the law into his own hands to take down a psychotic killer.

842) The Great Beauty

The Great Beauty is a visually stunning exploration of life, love, and the pursuit of meaning in modern Rome.

843) Bonnie and Clyde

Bonnie and Clyde is a classic crime drama about two young lovers on a crime spree across the United States during the Great Depression.

844) Detachment

Detachment is a drama about a substitute teacher who attempts to inspire a disconnected and disinterested student body while struggling to find a meaningful connection in his own life.

845) This Is England

This Is England is a coming-of-age drama set in the Thatcher era, exploring the struggles of a young boy as he navigates the harsh realities of life in a small English town.

846) Kung Fu Hustle

Kung Fu Hustle is a comedic martial arts action film about a hapless con artist who must use his wits and kung fu skills to save a poor village from the Axe Gang.

847) The Color Purple

The Color Purple is a powerful drama about an African-American woman's journey to self-discovery and acceptance.

848) Malcolm X

Malcolm X is a biographical drama about the African-American activist's life and legacy, focusing on his transformation from street hustler to Muslim minister and leader of the civil rights movement.

849) Ray

Ray is a biopic about the life of the legendary musician Ray Charles, showing the struggles he faced while overcoming personal and professional obstacles to become one of the most influential artists of all time.

850) The Name of the Rose

The Name of the Rose is a mystery drama set in a 14th-century monastery, where a monk and his novice investigate a series of suspicious deaths.

851) Fantastic Planet

Fantastic Planet is a French animated science fiction film about a world where humans are kept as pets by an alien race of giants.

852) Belle de Jour

Belle de Jour is a surrealist drama about a bored housewife who takes up work as a prostitute in a high-end brothel while her husband remains unaware.

853) Finding Neverland

Finding Neverland is a heartwarming movie about how the power of imagination and friendship can help bring hope and joy to those who need it.

854) Ordinary People

Ordinary People is a drama about a family struggling to cope with the death of their older son and the resulting emotional turmoil.

855) South Park: Bigger, Longer & Uncut

South Park: Bigger, Longer & Uncut is a satirical musical comedy film about four boys who sneak into an R-rated movie and must save the world from a demonic conspiracy.

856) The Last Emperor

The Last Emperor follows the life of Pu Yi, the last emperor of China, from his coronation in 1908 to his death in 1967.

857) Paprika

Paprika is an animated psychological thriller about a group of scientists trying to use a machine that can enter people's dreams to help them overcome their psychological problems.

858) Miller's Crossing

Miller's Crossing is a gangster film set in the 1930s about a man caught between two rival gangs who must make a difficult decision to save his friends.

859) Perfect Strangers

Perfect Strangers is a romantic comedy about a couple who agree to exchange partners to spice up their relationship, only to find themselves falling in love with each other.

860) Badlands

Badlands is a 1973 crime drama film about a teenage girl and her older boyfriend who go on a killing spree across the Midwest.

861) Zulu

Zulu is a historical war drama about the Battle of Rorke's Drift during the Anglo-Zulu War, in which a small British garrison successfully defends against an overwhelming attack by a Zulu army.

862) Open Your Eyes

Open Your Eyes is a psychological thriller that follows a young man who attempts to piece together his past after a disfiguring accident leaves him questioning reality.

863) Me and Earl and the Dying Girl

Me and Earl and the Dying Girl is a coming-of-age story about a teenage boy and his unlikely friendship with a classmate who is battling cancer.

864) Waking Life

Waking Life is a rotoscoped, philosophical exploration of the nature of reality, dreams, and the meaning of life.

865) The Wind Rises

The Wind Rises is an animated drama about an engineer's dream of creating a beautiful airplane and his struggles to make it a reality.

866) Run Lola Run

Run Lola Run is a German film about a woman's desperate race against time to save her boyfriend's life.

867) The Quiet Man

The Quiet Man is a romantic comedy-drama about an American man who returns to his Irish hometown to reclaim his family's land and find love.

868) Kubo and the Two Strings

Kubo and the Two Strings is an animated fantasy adventure about a young boy on a quest to save his family and defeat the Moon King and his evil sisters.

869) Breathless

Breathless is a French New Wave classic about a young criminal's tumultuous relationship with a young woman, as he tries to evade the police.

870) Fantasia

Fantasia is an animated film featuring classical music and colorful visuals that tells stories through music and animation.

871) Nebraska

Nebraska is a bittersweet comedy-drama about an aging father and his son's journey across the Midwest in search of a million-dollar sweepstakes prize.

872) Beasts of No Nation

Beasts of No Nation tells the story of a child soldier in an unnamed West African country who struggles to survive and find his way in a world of violence and chaos.

873) The Man from Nowhere

The Man from Nowhere follows an ex-special agent who embarks on a mission to protect a young girl from the clutches of a ruthless drug gang.

874) Black Book

Black Book is a suspenseful and thrilling World War II drama about a Dutch Jewish woman's dangerous mission to infiltrate the Nazi regime and help the Dutch resistance.

875) The Double Life of Véronique

The Double Life of VÃ©ronique is a mysterious and surreal exploration of identity, love, and destiny.

876) Short Cuts

Short Cuts is a 1993 American comedy-drama film directed by Robert Altman that follows the intersecting lives of 22 characters in Los Angeles.

877) Night on Earth

Night on Earth follows five different taxi drivers in five different cities as they each experience a unique night of comedy, drama, and insight.

878) The Vanishing

The Vanishing is a psychological thriller about a man's obsessive search for his missing girlfriend, and the terrifying consequences of his quest.

879) A Man for All Seasons

A Man for All Seasons is a 1966 British historical drama film about Sir Thomas More's struggle to remain true to his conscience while serving as Lord Chancellor of England during the reign of Henry VIII.

880) Good Bye Lenin!

Good Bye Lenin! is a comedic drama about a family in East Germany who must keep up a charade to protect their mother from the shock of the reunification of Germany.

881) Porco Rosso

Porco Rosso is an animated fantasy adventure film about an aging World War I fighter pilot who has been transformed into a pig and must battle sky pirates to save his beloved homeland.

882) Invasion of the Body Snatchers

Invasion of the Body Snatchers is a sci-fi horror film about an alien species that takes over the bodies and minds of humans in order to create a perfect, emotionless society.

883) Confessions

Confessions is a psychological thriller about a teacher seeking revenge against the students who killed her daughter.

884) The Little Prince

The Little Prince is an animated fantasy adventure film about a young girl who meets an eccentric aviator and embarks on a journey of discovery to a magical world of imagination.

885) The Broken Circle Breakdown

The Broken Circle Breakdown is a heart-wrenching drama about a couple struggling to cope with the loss of their daughter while trying to keep their relationship alive.

886) The Motorcycle Diaries

The Motorcycle Diaries is a biographical film about the journey of a young Ernesto 'Che' Guevara and his friend Alberto Granado as they travel across South America on a motorcycle.

887) The African Queen

The African Queen is a classic adventure romance film set in Africa during World War I, following two mismatched characters as they travel down a river in a small boat.

888) Wait Until Dark

Wait Until Dark follows a blind woman as she is terrorized by criminals searching for a mysterious doll they believe is in her apartment.

889) Scarface

Scarface is a classic gangster drama about a Cuban refugee's rise to power in 1980s Miami.

890) When Marnie Was There

When Marnie Was There is an animated coming-of-age story about a young girl who discovers a mysterious connection between herself and a mysterious girl who appears to be living in a nearby abandoned mansion.

891) Cape Fear

Cape Fear is a psychological thriller about a convicted rapist seeking revenge on the lawyer who helped put him in jail.

892) Hedwig and the Angry Inch

Hedwig and the Angry Inch is a musical comedy-drama about a genderqueer East German singer-songwriter navigating a rocky road to self-discovery and acceptance.

893) Happy Together

Happy Together is a drama about a couple struggling to maintain their relationship while living in Buenos Aires.

894) Hard Boiled

Hard Boiled is an action-packed crime drama following a maverick cop as he attempts to take down a ruthless criminal syndicate.

895) Black Narcissus

Black Narcissus is a psychological drama about a group of nuns who struggle to maintain their faith and sanity while living in a remote palace in the Himalayas.

896) Jules and Jim

Jules and Jim is a French New Wave classic about two close friends, their shared love for the same woman, and the effects of their relationship on all three of them.

897) Taste of Cherry

Taste of Cherry is a film about a man who searches for someone to help him commit suicide and the conversations he has with the people he meets along the way.

898) The Salesman

The Salesman is a drama about a married couple whose relationship is tested when the wife is assaulted in their new home.

899) Adam's Apples

Adam's Apples is a dark comedy about a neo-nazi who forms an unlikely bond with a priest while doing community service at a local church.

900) Frost/Nixon

Frost/Nixon is a 2008 biographical drama film about the 1977 television interviews between British journalist David Frost and former U.S. President Richard Nixon.

901) Down by Law

Down by Law is a comedy-drama about three unlikely friends who find themselves in jail together and must work together to escape.

902) The Triplets of Belleville

The Triplets of Belleville is an animated comedy-adventure about a grandmother and her beloved grandson who embark on a wild and offbeat journey to rescue him from kidnappers.

903) Joint Security Area

Joint Security Area is a South Korean thriller about two investigators who uncover a hidden truth behind a shooting incident that occurred at a border between North and South Korea.

904) Dreams

Dreams is a series of surrealistic short films directed by Akira Kurosawa that explore the depths of the human subconscious.

905) After the Wedding

After the Wedding is a drama about two women who discover the truth about their lives and the secrets of their pasts when one of them is invited to attend a wedding.

906) Evil

Evil is a horror film about a group of people who must confront a supernatural force when they become trapped in a mysterious house.

907) The Experiment

The Experiment is a psychological thriller about a group of people who volunteer for a two-week social experiment that quickly turns into a battle for survival.

908) Key Largo

Key Largo is a classic gangster film set in post-war Florida, featuring Humphrey Bogart as a war veteran facing off against a mobster played by Edward G. Robinson.

909) The Caine Mutiny

In The Caine Mutiny, a US Navy lieutenant relieves a captain of his command during a typhoon, leading to a court-martial for mutiny.

910) In America

In America is a heartfelt drama about an immigrant family struggling to make a new life in New York City while dealing with the loss of a loved one.

911) The Magdalene Sisters

The Magdalene Sisters is a powerful drama about three young Irish women who are sent to a convent for rehabilitation after being labeled ""fallen women"" by their conservative society.

912) Joyeux Noel

Joyeux Noel is a heart-warming story about a group of World War I soldiers who temporarily lay down their arms on Christmas Eve in 1914 to share a moment of peace and humanity.

913) The Girl Who Leapt Through Time

The Girl Who Leapt Through Time is a sci-fi drama about a teenage girl who discovers she has the ability to time travel and must use it to fix her mistakes and save the people she loves.

914) The Muppet Christmas Carol

The Muppet Christmas Carol is a fun and heartwarming musical retelling of Charles Dickens' classic tale of redemption and the true meaning of Christmas.

915) The Breadwinner

The Breadwinner is an animated film about a young Afghan girl who disguises herself as a boy in order to provide for her family after her father's arrest.

916) The Purple Rose of Cairo

The Purple Rose of Cairo is a romantic comedy-drama about a woman who falls in love with a character from a movie who steps out of the screen into her world.

917) My Life as a Zucchini

My Life as a Zucchini is an endearing and heartwarming story about a young orphan's journey to find a place to belong.

918) Fireworks

Fireworks is a coming-of-age drama about three teenage boys who are struggling to find their place in the world and discover the power of friendship.

919) Love and Death

Love and Death is a 1975 comedy film directed by Woody Allen, which follows a cowardly Russian soldier's attempts to find love and avoid death during Napoleon's invasion of Russia.

920) The Past

The Past is a drama about a woman who must confront her estranged husband when he returns to France to finalize their divorce after four years of separation.

921) Zelig

Zelig is a mockumentary about a mysterious man who can transform himself to blend in with any group of people, leading to a media frenzy.

922) The Edge of Heaven

The Edge of Heaven is a poignant drama about the intersecting lives of a Turkish family and a German widow, and the consequences of their intertwined destinies.

923) Once Upon a Time in Hollywood

Once Upon a Time in Hollywood follows the story of an aging actor and his stunt double as they navigate the changing landscape of Hollywood in 1969.

924) Harry Potter and the Sorcerer's Stone

Harry Potter embarks on a magical journey as he discovers his true identity and destiny as a wizard when he attends Hogwarts School of Witchcraft and Wizardry.

925) American Psycho

American Psycho is a darkly comic satire about a wealthy investment banker who descends into a nightmarish world of depraved violence and psychopathic behavior.

926) Sicario

Sicario is an intense crime drama that follows an idealistic FBI agent as she is enlisted by a government task force to aid in the escalating war against drugs along the US-Mexico border.

927) RoboCop

RoboCop is a sci-fi action movie about a cyborg police officer who fights crime and corruption in a dystopian futuristic Detroit.

928) The Fifth Element

The Fifth Element is an action-packed sci-fi adventure set in a futuristic world where a cab driver must save the universe from destruction by an evil force.

929) Searching

Searching is a suspenseful thriller that follows a father's desperate search for his missing daughter, using the technology of the digital age to find her.

930) Superbad

Superbad is a coming-of-age comedy about two high school friends on a quest to buy alcohol for a party, and the misadventures they get into along the way.

931) A Star Is Born

A Star Is Born is a romantic musical drama about a rising singer-songwriter who falls in love with an established musician and their tumultuous relationship.

932) Guardians of the Galaxy Vol. 2

Guardians of the Galaxy Vol. 2 follows the Guardians as they unravel the mystery of Peter Quill's true parentage while fighting to keep their newfound family together.

933) 300

300 is an action-packed historical fantasy about a small group of Spartan warriors led by King Leonidas who battle against the overwhelming forces of the Persian Empire.

934) Office Space

Office Space is a comedy about a group of disgruntled office workers who devise a plan to get even with their oppressive boss.

935) Moana

Moana is an animated musical adventure about a young girl who sets sail on a daring mission to save her people and find her own identity.

936) Watchmen

Watchmen is an action-packed superhero movie that follows a group of masked vigilantes as they uncover a conspiracy to destroy the world.

937) Minority Report

Minority Report is a sci-fi action thriller about a police department that uses psychic technology to try to prevent crime before it happens.

938) Kick-Ass

Kick-Ass is an action-comedy about an ordinary teenager who dons a superhero costume and attempts to fight crime and make a difference in the world.

939) Stardust

Stardust is a fantasy adventure film about a young man's journey to a magical kingdom to retrieve a fallen star in order to win the heart of the woman he loves.

940) Hell or High Water

Hell or High Water is a modern western crime drama that follows two brothers who resort to a desperate scheme in order to save their family's land.

941) Kung Fu Panda

Kung Fu Panda is an animated action-comedy about an unlikely panda who fulfills his destiny as the chosen one to save the Valley of Peace from a villainous snow leopard.

942) The Butterfly Effect

The Butterfly Effect is a psychological thriller about a man who discovers he has the power to travel back in time and alter his past, with unexpected and far-reaching consequences.

943) Saw

Saw is a horror movie about a sadistic killer who puts people in deadly traps in order to test their will to survive.

944) The Blind Side

The Blind Side is a heartwarming sports drama about a homeless teen who is taken in by a family and goes on to become a successful football player.

945) Moneyball

Moneyball is a movie about Oakland Athletics general manager Billy Beane and his attempt to put together a competitive baseball team on a limited budget by using sabermetrics.

946) Star Wars: Episode III - Revenge of the Sith

In Star Wars: Episode III - Revenge of the Sith, Anakin Skywalker's fall to the dark side of the Force is complete as he becomes Darth Vader and the Galactic Empire is born.

947) My Cousin Vinny

My Cousin Vinny is a comedy about a bumbling New York lawyer who must defend his cousin in a small-town Southern courtroom.

948) The Thin Red Line

The Thin Red Line is a war drama about a group of soldiers struggling with the psychological and physical effects of World War II as they fight in the Battle of Guadalcanal.

949) Inside Man

Inside Man is a crime thriller about a bank heist in which the mastermind must outwit a determined police detective and a power broker with a hidden agenda.

950) What We Do in the Shadows

What We Do in the Shadows is a mockumentary-style comedy about a group of vampires living together in modern-day Wellington, New Zealand.

951) Gone Baby Gone

Gone Baby Gone is a crime drama about two detectives who investigate the kidnapping of a four-year-old girl in the Boston neighborhood of Dorchester.

952) Mulan

Mulan is an animated Disney movie about a young Chinese girl who disguises herself as a man to take her elderly father's place in the Imperial Army and save her country from invaders.

953) True Grit

True Grit is a classic Western film about a young girl who seeks revenge for her father's murder with the help of a hardened U.S. Marshal.

954) The Fly

The Fly is a horror/sci-fi film about a scientist whose teleportation experiment goes wrong, resulting in a human-fly hybrid.

955) The Royal Tenenbaums

The Royal Tenenbaums is a dark comedy-drama about a dysfunctional family of former child prodigies struggling to reconnect and reconcile.

956) Despicable Me

Despicable Me follows the story of a supervillain who unexpectedly adopts three orphan girls and learns the importance of family.

957) Dark City

Dark City is a neo-noir science fiction film about a man who discovers he is part of an experiment to alter the memories of a group of people living in a mysterious city.

958) Close Encounters of the Third Kind

Close Encounters of the Third Kind is a science fiction movie about a group of people who attempt to make contact with alien life after experiencing various unexplained phenomena.

959) The Mitchells vs the Machines

The Mitchells must team up with the robots they were attempting to disconnect in order to save the world from a tech apocalypse.

960) Lethal Weapon

Lethal Weapon is an action-packed buddy cop movie following two mismatched LAPD detectives who must work together to take down a dangerous drug lord.

961) The Naked Gun: From the Files of Police Squad!

The Naked Gun: From the Files of Police Squad! is a zany comedy that follows the bumbling police lieutenant Frank Drebin as he attempts to foil a diabolical plot to assassinate the Queen of England.

962) Eastern Promises

Eastern Promises is a crime drama that follows a midwife's journey as she unravels a dark mystery involving a dangerous Russian criminal family.

963) The Others

The Others is a psychological horror film about a family living in an isolated manor haunted by mysterious entities.

964) The Skin I Live In

The Skin I Live In tells the story of a brilliant plastic surgeon who creates a type of synthetic skin to help a burn victim, but his obsession leads to unexpected consequences.

965) The Birds

The Birds is a horror-thriller film about a small California town that is suddenly attacked by a flock of birds.

966) End of Watch

End of Watch is a thrilling and intense crime drama that follows two police officers as they fight crime on the streets of South Central Los Angeles.

967) The Raid: Redemption

The Raid: Redemption is an action-packed Indonesian martial arts film about a SWAT team's attempt to take down a notorious drug lord in a dangerous, crime-ridden apartment building.

968) Dark Waters

Dark Waters is a gripping legal drama that follows a tenacious lawyer as he uncovers a dark history of chemical pollution and its devastating effects on a small town.

969) The Road Warrior

The Road Warrior is a post-apocalyptic action-adventure film about a loner who helps protect a small community from a vicious gang of marauders.

970) The Jungle Book

The Jungle Book is a Disney classic about an orphaned boy named Mowgli who is raised by a pack of wolves and embarks on a journey of self-discovery.

971) Dawn of the Planet of the Apes

Dawn of the Planet of the Apes is a thrilling action-adventure film that follows a growing nation of genetically evolved apes led by Caesar, who is threatened by a band of human survivors of a devastating virus.

972) Die Hard with a Vengeance

Die Hard with a Vengeance is an action-packed thriller in which John McClane must team up with a shopkeeper to stop a mad bomber from destroying New York City.

973) Match Point

Match Point is a psychological thriller about a young tennis pro who will do whatever it takes to climb the social ladder.

974) Snow White and the Seven Dwarfs

Snow White and the Seven Dwarfs is a classic Disney animated movie about a princess who befriends seven dwarfs and is pursued by an evil queen.

975) Ponyo

Ponyo is an animated film about a goldfish princess who wants to become human and the friendship she forms with a human boy that helps her on her quest.

976) After Hours

After Hours is a dark comedy about a man's increasingly desperate and dangerous night in New York City.

977) 50/50

50/50 is a comedy-drama about a young man's journey to beat cancer while learning to appreciate life and the people around him.

978) 21 Grams

21 Grams follows the intertwined lives of three people connected by a tragic accident, exploring themes of love, loss, and redemption.

979) Seven Pounds

Seven Pounds is a drama about a man attempting to right the wrongs of his past by helping seven strangers in need.

980) From Here to Eternity

From Here to Eternity is a classic drama set in Hawaii during World War II, about the struggles of a group of individuals to find love and redemption in the face of war and prejudice.

981) Rushmore

Rushmore is a quirky coming-of-age comedy-drama about an eccentric 15-year-old Max Fischer, who attends the prestigious Rushmore Academy and navigates his way through a series of misadventures.

982) The Taking of Pelham One Two Three

The Taking of Pelham One Two Three is a thriller about a group of criminals hijacking a New York City subway train and demanding a ransom from the mayor.

983) Enter the Dragon

Enter the Dragon is a classic martial arts film starring Bruce Lee as a martial artist who enters an underground tournament to take down a crime lord.

984) The Last King of Scotland

The Last King of Scotland is a biographical drama about a young doctor from Scotland who becomes the personal physician of Ugandan dictator Idi Amin.

985) Rebel Without a Cause

Rebel Without a Cause is a classic coming-of-age drama about a troubled teen struggling to find his identity in a world of misunderstanding and alienation.

986) Sabrina

Sabrina is a romantic comedy about a wealthy playboy who falls in love with the daughter of his family's chauffeur.

987) The Bridges of Madison County

The Bridges of Madison County is a romantic drama about an Italian-American housewife who embarks on a passionate but ultimately doomed affair with a traveling photographer.

988) Barton Fink

Barton Fink is a dark comedy-drama about a playwright who struggles to write a wrestling picture while staying in a haunted hotel in 1940s Hollywood.

989) I Am Sam

I Am Sam is a heartwarming drama about a father's struggle to regain custody of his daughter with the help of a lawyer and some friends.

990) 25th Hour

25th Hour follows Monty Brogan as he faces his last 24 hours of freedom before going to prison for seven years.

991) United 93

United 93 is a dramatization of the events on board United Airlines Flight 93 on September 11, 2001, when passengers and crew attempted to take back control of the plane from hijackers.

992) The Odd Couple

The Odd Couple is a classic comedy about two mismatched roommates, the neat freak Felix and the slob Oscar, and their hilarious attempts to live together.

993) The Invisible Man

The Invisible Man is a sci-fi horror film about a scientist who uses his newly acquired invisibility to terrorize those who wronged him.

994) A Very Long Engagement

A Very Long Engagement is a romantic drama about a young woman's determined quest to find out what happened to her missing fiancÃ© during World War I.

995) Control

Control is a biopic about the life of British musician Ian Curtis, the lead singer of the band Joy Division, and his struggles with depression and epilepsy.

996) The Station Agent

The Station Agent is a heartwarming story about an unlikely friendship between an introverted train enthusiast, an artist, and a hot dog vendor.

997) Philomena

Philomena is a heartwarming drama about a woman's search for her long-lost son, which leads to unexpected revelations and a powerful bond of friendship.

998) Shine

Shine is a biographical drama about a young Australian pianist's struggle with mental illness and his journey to becoming a renowned concert pianist.

999) Eyes Without a Face

Eyes Without a Face is a 1960 French horror film about a mad scientist who attempts to restore the beauty of his daughter's disfigured face by any means necessary.

1000) Celda 211

Celda 211 is a Spanish prison drama about a man who must survive the harsh conditions of a maximum security prison while uncovering its secrets.

Made in United States
Troutdale, OR
04/24/2024

19430521R00111